BEING HUMAN

Gerry Pyves

SHI'ZEN PUBLICATIONS

Published by Shi'Zen Publications
www.shizen.co.uk

Printed by Swiftprint, Huddersfield

ISBN 978 0 9929375 0 8

THE PSYCHOLOGY OF CHANGE SERIES

BEING HUMAN

This book explains why we all do what we do, even when we don't want to. It explores the psychological roots of human behaviour and looks at how we can recognise and make changes at different levels of the human psyche. It explains our creative and destructive drives, the ego and the id and how at the root of all human failure and success lies our life script. It shows us how we can take greater charge of our lives and also why change sometimes doesn't work. It explains why we may have to dig deeper into the archeology of our psyche in order to be successful in life. This book lays down many of the psychological foundations for book two.

THE FAIRY TALE PHENOMENON

This book explores the immense power of our unconscious and shows how we can use this information to identify our life scripts. It gives many examples of the power of story and metaphor in healing the mind and explains why some of the greatest minds in human history were obsessed with fairy tales and myths. It seems that at the heart of our happiness lies the story we tell ourselves. It explains why, if we want to change this narrative, we must speak to our unconscious in its own language - the language of fairy tales.

TRANSFORMING LIVES

This book guides you through the twelve practical steps needed to actually change your life's narrative through *The Fairy Tale Process*. This is a dynamic and exciting new approach to personal transformation that anyone can use. It gives us direct access to the vast power of our unconscious mind. It signifies a revolution in the way that we can each transform our lives and uses some of the newest and most practical tools of psychotherapy to do this. Each step is accompanied by extensive notes for both the public and the professional. With this book, you can harness the vast forces of your unconscious mind and use them to transform your life.

I dedicate this book to my three children, Laurie, Hannah and Alfie who I love more than life itself, despite any appearances to the contrary.

AMOR VINCIT OMNIA

CONTENTS

FOREWORD   9

INTRODUCTION: ALL LIFE IS ENERGY   11

CREATIVE AND DESTRUCTIVE ENERGY   15

REALITY   19

THE SELF AND OTHERS   25

MASTERING UNCONSCIOUS URGES   29

THE EGO AND THE ID   33

UNDERSTANDING PSYCHOTHERAPY   37

A MAP TO NAVIGATE WITH   43

THE THREE EGO STATES   47

THE FLOW OF ENERGY - Cathexis   57

WHO'S RUNNING THE SHOW?   63

STIMULUS HUNGER   67

THE FIVE HUMAN INTERACTIONS   75

LIFE SCRIPT   87

A VERY OLD IDEA...   91

THE LOCATION OF LIFE SCRIPT   95

HOW LIFE SCRIPT EVOLVED   99

DANGEROUS URGES   105

WHY WE ALL DO WHAT WE DO...   109

NOTES FOR THE CURIOUS   115

BIBLIOGRAPHY   133

FOREWORD

Eric Berne, the founder of Transactional Analysis, maintained that we are living out our lives according to a life plan written by a three year old. The aim of this book is to establish some of the basic psychological forces at play within the human psyche. It seeks to answer that most fundamental of questions, "Why do we all do what we do, even when we don't want to?"

A great deal of "success literature" seems to think we can manage without this information. We can't. To properly understand how to succeed in life, we need to properly understand just what being human means. We need to appreciate some of the tectonic forces at play within the human psyche. Only then can we come up with effective models for navigating our way through life successfully.

This book is also a crash course in some of the key psychological ideas of the last two hundred years. There is a particular emphasis on Transactional Analysis, which I believe to be one of the most accessible models for understanding humans. It is also well proven, with over fifty years of clinical effectiveness under its belt. There are thousands of educators, organisation leaders and therapists using Transactional Analysis effectively, worldwide.

The aim here is to provide a simple, clear and practical summary of some very complex ideas. Only by knowing these basic concepts can we be sufficiently well informed to make effective changes to our lives. If you are interested in understanding how your success in life relates to how the human psyche works, then this book is for you.

More information about these complex ideas is provided in the notes section and bibliography at the back of this book.

1

INTRODUCTION:

ALL LIFE IS ENERGY

"The energy
of the mind is
the essence
of life"
– *Aristotle*

All life is energy. This energy only has one aim; to find balance. In the body we call this balance *Homeostasis,* as when we perspire to bring down our temperature. The excess tension of too much body heat is *discharged* through the formation of water and the subsequent cooling that happens. Through this water evaporating, the air around us absorbs this energy and actually warms up a tiny amount. No energy is lost. It just *transforms.* This is a fundamental law of nature and it applies to the human psyche, too.

In nature, we call this balance and transformation of energy, *weather.* Hot air rises simply to find balance and cool itself. This upwards movement also causes cool air to rush in and balance out the gap left at ground level. The tension created by that hot air rising is *discharged* through the roaring hurricane that ensues at ground level.

Another example from nature would be the lightning bolt. A bolt of lightning simply seeks to balance the vast electrical charges of the earth and sky. The tension of all the negative ions in the sky is *discharged* through the release of the lightning bolt and equilibrium is restored. Discharge is a fundamental phenomenon of nature; it is also a fundamental principle of the human mind.

In society we call this balance of energy, *government.* Through government, the different tensions within society seek to find their natural expression or *discharge.* Some do this through the ballot box and some do it through rioting or the gun. Between societies we call this *international relations,* as different countries seek to find their balance of energy with each other, globally. Some do this through trade and embassies and some do it through war. It is all about *the discharge of energy,* whether it is done through polite conversation at an embassy dinner or through the magazine of a rifle.

In relationships we call this balance *sex,* as when the male energy seeks to find balance with the female energy and vice versa. Some do this through loving relationships and others do it through violence and rape. Again, it is all about *discharge*.

Within the mind, we call this movement of energy *cathexis*. Cathexis describes how psychic energy moves from one part of the mind to another which then controls how we think, feel and behave. Tensions build up within us and the energy moves as we seek to find a way to *discharge* this excess energy into the environment.

For example, a growing energy of rage may build up as a result of being ignored by those around us. That energy must go somewhere. Instead of keeping it "suppressed" in a part of my mind, I *cathect* it to another part of my mind that initiates action. Consequently, I may decide to go to the gym and pump iron furiously until the energy has been *discharged* into the environment, safely. Socially, we call this "letting off steam." What we are doing is *discharging* the excess energy within our psyche into the environment, perhaps by hitting a punch bag.

Likewise, if we feel grief and despair because a loved one has died or we just got jilted then we must *discharge* this excess energy by crying or wailing into a pillow. If we had a frightening experience then we may need to *discharge* the energy of our fear through uncontrollable shaking. If we are happy, then we must *discharge* that build up of energy into the environment, through laughter and dance. This is no different to the excess heat in our body being *discharged* into the environment through sweating.

Some people do this psychic *discharge* well, which we call success, health and happiness. Others do it less well, which we call failure, illness and misery. If, instead of hitting a punch bag down the local gym, I deal with my building rage with alcohol I may find myself in a drunken brawl. The following day I may nurse a hangover and a broken wrist. I may even find myself in prison on a charge of manslaughter. The only difference between the man in prison and the man out with his family happily walking down the shopping mall the next day, is how each *discharged* their energy. Success, health and happiness are simply about our psychic energy and how we manage to *discharge* that energy.

The power of the human mind is awesome. Most traditions of psychology talk of powerful forces at play within the mind. They may use different languages, but most agree that there are vast subterranean and tectonic forces at play. Since the time of Freud, most psychological professionals have agreed that life consists of the discharge of just two primal forces. These are the two forces that drive all human behaviour. Simply put, they are the energies of creating and destroying, or as the Greeks put it, *Eros* and *Thanatos*, love and death.

Just how we deal with these two energies is what this book is all about.

2

CREATIVE AND DESTRUCTIVE ENERGY

"Most of this creative and destructive energy lives in our unconscious mind."

It is possible to view all human behaviour as doing one of two things; creating or destroying. Humans can be seen building things, helping and supporting each other and having loving and intimate relationships with each other. We will call this *The Creative Principle*.

Human beings can also be seen demolishing things, fighting and arguing with each other, abusing and killing each other. We will call this *The Destructive Principle*. *The Destructive Principle* can be clearly seen across societies as well as individuals. It can be seen in the actions of the murderer, in the violence of war and in the self harming of individuals who drink excessively, smoke or cut themselves.

The Destructive Principle can be seen in the actions of the boxer, the work of the prosecutor, in social and political revolutions and war. *The Destructive Principle* is largely about arguing and fighting, ending relationships and destroying things. When human interactions result in damaging and harmful outcomes, this is the psychic force at play.

The Creative Principle can be seen in the actions of the lover, the work of the healer, in the trade between nations and in the self healing actions of individuals who become carers, go out jogging or work out in the gym. *The Creative Principle* is about building relationships and community. When human interaction ends up in a creative and productive outcome, this is the psychic force at play.

**Most of this creative and destructive energy lives in our unconscious mind,
completely out of our awareness.**

These two *unconscious* forces can be clearly seen in the behaviour of young children. One minute they are destroying their environment and fighting others and in the next they are playing creatively and behaving in a loving manner. Young children have not yet learned to restrain these forces with their *conscious* mind. This is one reason they are such fun to watch and be around.

The challenge of being human is to find the safest routes for the discharge of these two powerful unconscious forces.

As children we soon learn that in order to gratify our wishes without getting into trouble we must control these urges. We learn to control them and wait. This waiting will build up the tension within the psyche, rather like a volcano building up to an eruption. In order to control and manage this discharge safely in a way that does not threaten our survival, we develop our conscious mind. This is called "growing up."

As we grow up, our conscious mind learns to control the discharge of both *creative* and *destructive* energies in a way that fits with the reality of life around us. Some people do this well and end up happy and successful. Others do not, and end up miserable and unsuccessful.

In order to release the build up of tension created by these two primal urges, we must find a way to satisfy them which does not threaten our own survival. Just how we decide to manage these two primal urges is what constitutes the unique aspects of our personality. It is why Joe is different from John and Jane is different to Jemima. To do well in life, we must find a way to discharge our unconscious urges in a way that fits in with how things actually work in real life. This is one of the simplest definitions of success.

Success can be defined as our ability to discharge the powerful forces within our psyche in a way that works with the reality of the world in which we live.

To sum up then, one way to view being human is to see us as comprising two primal energies which are competing with each other. These are called *The Creative Principle* and *The Destructive Principle*. Each requires discharge whenever the build up of energy reaches a critical level. Our conscious mind controls how and when we discharge this volcanic energy. The more our discharge of energy fits in with the reality of how the world actually works, the happier and more successful we are likely to be.

So just what is this reality that we must "fit" into?

3

REALITY

"If our early experiences in life gave us warped pictures of the reality of either ourselves, others, or the world, then we are in serious trouble..."

Whilst philosophers can luxuriate in endless discussions about the exact nature of reality, those of us in the psychological professions must simply deal with what works in the world. The people we work with desire only to function better and thus become happier and healthier. Our definition of success is simply what "works" in the society we live in. It should be remembered that very often what works in one society does not work in another, so nothing is absolute, here.

We have already seen that to be successful, healthy and happy in life, our conscious mind must find effective ways to discharge the powerful urges of our unconscious in a way that works in the world. If we fail in this endeavour then we will mostly end up "mad, bad or sad." Some may end up in psychiatric wards (mad), whilst others may end up in prison (bad). Many others may simply walk around in a state of depression (sad).

This is no small thing, this reality business. We are dealing here with nothing other than life and death. At its extreme, the "bad" may sabotage their lives and the lives of those around them through the violence of homicide. The "sad" may end up tragically killing themselves and traumatising all those around them. The "mad" (if they have not already done so), may end up in such an extreme state of psychosis that no one can help them find their way back to reality. The three options of killing others, killing self or going mad are the three "escape hatches" through which we may have decided at any early age to remove ourselves from life, if the going gets tough. Such options are commonplace and are a matter of historical record in hospital wards and prisons all over the world.

As we shall see later on in the book, sometimes such options lie hidden deep within the mind. Yet how many of us have held conscious fantasies of either harming ourselves, harming others or just "flipping out"? Such moments may indicate the possible existence of a hidden decision to jump down one of these three escape hatches "if the going gets tough."

Identifying such escape hatches and helping clients close them is the first priority of any psychological professional. This is why all psychotherapy is at root a life and death matter.

Such escape hatches are held as an action of last resort. We close them in two ways: Firstly we make a conscious decision that, no matter what the circumstances "I will not either hurt myself or kill myself in any way, accidentally or on purpose and I will not set it up for anyone else to do it to me." Such decisions are then framed in the positive by stating that "I will live a healthy and full life and promote the same in others." Secondly we find out just what aspect of our map of reality is skew and then put it right, so we don't ever need to travel down such paths of last resort.

To avoid this fate "of last resort" and be successful in life, we must contend with three different aspects of reality:
The World, Others and The Self.

Living and living well simply means coming up with accurate pictures of the world. Successful farmers build up accurate pictures of how nature works (*The World*). This means they are able to manipulate reality to grow crops successfully. Successful farmers can also build accurate pictures of how people behave (*Others*). This means they can predict what crops people actually want and then supply them.

Successful farmers also build up an accurate picture of how their mind and body works (*The Self*). This means they can stay healthy and work effectively. Success in life simply depends on the accuracy of the pictures that we have built up about these three areas of life; the world, others and the self.

If our early experiences in life gave us warped pictures of the
reality of either ourselves, others, or the world we live in,
then we are in serious trouble.

The picture of reality that we carry around inside our heads is something that was actually painted by us at a very early age. Most of us are then faithfully married and fixed to this idea for the rest of our lives. This means that a great deal of our success in life actually comes down to the pictures we painted about the way the world works, at the age of three or four years old. Such pictures were based on the environment we were born into. Yet how well does the family environment that we grew up in, fit the world that we are actually living in now?

This is the simple origin of most of our self sabotaging behaviours; inaccurate pictures of reality that we hold in our heads. Eric Berne called this unconscious part of us that is following a faulty map or picture of the world "a demon." He wrote "But in all human beings the demon persists, bringing sudden pleasure or grief." This is the source of all self sabotaging behaviour.

What most writers about the unconscious agree upon is that our unconscious largely dictates our behaviour when it comes to dealing with reality. This means learning how to influence and direct our unconscious mind is an essential part of successful living. The more we can "fit" our discharge of these unconscious energies into the way our world is working now, the more successful our lives become.

Directing our unconscious urges in a healthy way may be the difference between helping others instead of harming them. It could mean the difference between contributing to life instead of becoming a burden on others through insanity. It could make the difference between living to a contented and ripe old age and killing ourselves prematurely.

Whether we see it at such extreme moments or at earlier and less dramatic stages beforehand, it all comes down to the way we discharge our energy into the world. The tragedy of most of our dysfunctional behaviour is that it is simply attempting to use behaviours that worked in the world we lived in at age three. For healthy living, we need to be able to update these habitual behaviours to ways that work in the world we are living in now.

Before we learn about the tools we can use to do this, we need to delve more deeply into how the human psyche actually works...

4

THE SELF AND OTHERS

"It is all about mastering our unconscious urges..."

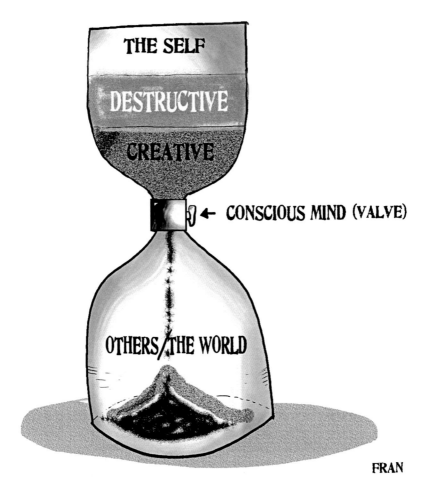

FRAN

The top section of this egg timer represents *The Self*. The bottom section represents *Others* and *The World*. It is primarily in relation to *The Self* that most errors in our pictures regarding reality are made. This is not surprising, as the unconscious forces of our destructive and creative energies remain largely invisible to us. The behaviour of *The World* and *Others* however is largely visible. This is also true for most of the *physical aspects* of the body. They are largely visible to us. This is not so for the internal workings of our mind.

The workings of our unconscious mind are almost completely invisible to us. One way to look at this is to regard our conscious mind as a valve that sits between the immense and largely unknown forces of our unconscious *Self*, controlling the discharge of those forces into the reality of *The World* and *Others*, as in the diagram.

Our conscious mind does its best to make judgments (or guesses) about the hidden inner tensions and urges within *The Self*. It then judges the state of the energy systems outside it by observing *Others* and *The World*. It then guides us in the best way to satisfy our need to discharge both our destructive and creative energies. It does this in a way that is most advantageous to our success in life. If no successful discharge is possible, then we must suppress and store this energy so that we can discharge it later.

The trouble with suppression is this: if we store too much energy for too long, we end up doing strange and inexplicable things. We find ourselves driving into trees whilst drunk, or sleeping with the boss. Perhaps we develop strange physical symptoms that have no medical explanation. If it gets really bad, then we develop what the psychological professionals call either *neurosis* or *psychosis*. All *neurosis* and all *psychosis* are simply the result of the our failure to discharge the pent-up energy of our creative and destructive urges. Consequently, this results in strange behaviours and inexplicable bodily symptoms.

Because society mostly condemns the raw display of either our creative or destructive energy as anti-social, we must either alter their expression or postpone them until they can be discharged safely. This means we must find more sophisticated and acceptable ways to express our urges. There are a variety of different ways we can do this. Mostly, we engage in light hearted "banter." This is where we can often see the famous freudian slip, where what we really mean slips out. Sometimes we discharge our urges inwardly instead of outwardly:

Inward Destructive:
"I can't strangle my daughter, so I will turn it on myself with a throat infection, instead."

Inward Creative:
"I can't have sex with my teacher, so I will have erotic dreams about her, instead."

Mostly, we use displacement. Instead of strangling a loved one, a clearly unacceptable urge, we write novels about people getting strangled. We still get to express the desire for strangulation, but displace the *object* of our strangulation. The news tells us daily of people who have failed to achieve such displacement with the actual people in their lives. One study showed that 80% of all murders are committed by someone who is known to the victim. This explains why those closest to the victim are the first suspects of any murder investigation by the police.

Which is why, instead of committing murder, we might write about strangulation. We have also done something else that is clever, here. We have not only displaced the *object* of our fury, but we have displaced the *physical act* into a *literary one*. The most famous example of this literary displacement is Dante, who turned his love for Beatrice into a literary and spiritual act instead of a physical one. This is probably just as well, because Beatrice had no idea who Dante even was.

So when we displace our unconscious urges, we can displace *the object* of our urges or we can change *the activity*, or both. In addition to this, there is also *time displacement*. I might want to murder my boss, or the person driving the car in front of me, but I suppress such Mortido rage until 3pm next Saturday afternoon, when I can join 20,000 other people at my local football club in shouting *murderously* at the referee. First I suppress and store the energy. Then I translate it into a different activity (shouting not killing) and then I translate it into a different object (the referee instead of my boss). This is how most of us manage our unconscious urges. Learning how to do this is what growing up is all about.

As a teenager, I may wish to have sex with my teacher, a socially unacceptable behaviour that is often on the front pages of newspapers because of its catastrophic consequences. So instead, I suppress this desire until I am passing a florist and I bring my teacher a bunch of flowers as a gift. The person or "love object" remains the same, but the activity was changed or displaced from having sex into giving flowers.

It is all about mastering our unconscious urges…

5

MASTERING UNCONSCIOUS URGES

"This is the foundation stone of all successful human behaviour."

FRAN

In modern day society, our failure to successfully master the discharge of such primitive creative and destructive urges generally results in imprisonment or in the use of either legal or illegal drugs.

If we discharge this energy in bizarre and unacceptable ways, society calls us "mentally ill" and generally administers drugs to incapacitate and control us. If our behaviour means we break the laws of the land, then society calls us "criminals" and puts us into prison to incapacitate and control us. If we find ourselves managing badly in life, sometimes we incapacitate ourselves by self- administering recreational drugs. Thus it is that many people considerately save society both the burden and the cost of controlling and incapacitating them.

In this way, we can see that mastering and managing our postponement or displacement of discharge is the foundation stone of almost all successful human behaviour and interaction.

Learning how to master this discharge of energy is basically what our childhood is all about. During childhood, we derive much satisfaction from our growing mastery over the primitive destructive and creative forces of *The Self*. We derive much pleasure from controlling their release in our interaction with *The World* and *Others*. Whether it is pleasure from mastering our body in learning to swim, or from mastering the environment as in building a toy car, or in mastering our friends through kindness or bullying.

This is where we hit the thorny issue of our childhood playing a big part in controlling the way we behave today. If a person grows up in a dysfunctional family where it is quite normal to physically hit each other whenever they don't get what they want or need then this is likely to be their "default setting" when under stress in later adult life. At the time, as a grown up, this person feels that what they did was "right" when they punched a policeman who was trying to stop them from having fun. Much later on however, when he is sitting in the prison cell, this person then reflects that perhaps this was not such a good idea after all. It felt the natural and obvious thing to do at the time. It was an instinctive response. It is what he grew up doing, and neither parents nor teachers were able to convince him otherwise.

When we respond to situations in this automatic and instinctive way, we are most likely to display our destructive and creative urges. This is why so many artists and creative "types" also have a reputation for behaving rather badly. The classic example of this would be the famous behaviour of Rock and Roll bands during the 1970s, wrecking hotel rooms on tour and destroying guitars on stage. Such raw displays of child-like destructive urges were generally cheered on by the crowd who displaced their own destructive urges by identifying with the performer and mentally "smashed the guitar" with him.

Such instinctive and habitual behaviours generally "feel right" at the time. It is often only later on, when we start to reflect on the consequences of our actions, that we begin to wonder just how much choice there really was in that particular behaviour.

Whenever we behave in a way that damages a loved one, ruins our career prospects or compromises our health, we are dealing with our unconscious urges being channelled in a way that may have worked when we were young. The main problem is the mismatch between what we learned in our childhood and what works now. What we learned when we were young became habitual and entered into our unconscious mind. That is why it is instinctive and *feels right* at the time.

31

We are remarkably young when working out our ideas about what does and does not work in life. Most modern research into the brain now shows that these same early years are precisely the time when we are forming most of our neural channels. Our brains become hard wired to certain behaviours, based on our early experiences and beliefs. This is why, in later life, we can sometimes hit problems and start to find ourselves in the "same old, same old." We are still following patterns of thought, feeling and behaviour that were established in a very different environment to the situation we find ourselves in today.

Luckily, there is a part of the psyche that is susceptible to suggestions about making changes to the way we discharge our urges....it is called the ego.

6

THE EGO AND THE ID

"Psychoanalysts call this unconscious part of us The Id."

The Ego is the part of us that seeks to master our unconscious creative and destructive urges and channel their discharge into our environment. A great deal of pleasure is derived from doing this successfully, and much pain from failure. The best way to understand *The Ego* is to imagine that when we were very young, a small parcel of our vast unconscious mind split off to form this organ of mastery; the conscious mind. This is when we bit the biblical apple and became aware.

For the first time we became aware of "I" as separate from everything and everyone else around us. Because this "I" is now conscious, the remainder of our energy became unconscious and hidden from us. Psychoanalysts call this unconscious part of us *The Id*, which is simply Greek for "it " After generations of elite university education, this is the best that the greatest minds in the psychiatric profession could come up with..."It." Brilliant.

The garden of Eden, our early childhood state of unified wholeness, suddenly became hidden to us. We became separate from our *Id*.

The oneness and harmony that we experienced in the first year of life was sacrificed upon the altar of awareness. It was replaced by our delight in this new mastery over ourselves, others and the world.

This is why we often describe the forces of our conscious mind and our unconscious mind as being "at war" with each other. Our conscious awareness created a split in ourselves. We could no longer experience oneness with the world. We became separate. We were cast out of the garden of Eden and the gates were firmly locked. It's the price we pay for being different to animals, who show no such conscious self awareness. Only rarely are horses and dogs found reading Wittgenstein to understand their place in the world.

The trouble with our unconscious *Id* is that it wishes to gratify its urges *instantly* without any reference to the outside world. The conscious mind must therefore find ways to control these urges in order to discharge them in a way that ensures harmony with our environment. Berne writes, *"The reason that life is so difficult is that the Ego is in such a difficult situation. It has three forces to contend with, control and finally pull together for the satisfaction and safety of the individual: the Id instincts, the forces of nature, and other people."*

Whilst most of us are fully aware of the reality of nature and the reality of the people around us, only rarely do we acknowledge the reality of *the Id*. The force and power of our unconscious is like an elephant that is sitting in the middle of our sitting room. We can smell it, we must feed it, we must clear out its dung throughout the day. In fact it dominates our existence, yet nobody likes to talk about it. Many people even walk around denying the very existence of elephants.

Only when something goes badly wrong, say when the settee collapses under the weight of the elephant, do we talk about it or try and understand it. Only when people have problems in life or have mental breakdowns do they seek help from people who believe in the existence of elephants. These "elephant believers" are called personal coaches, mentors, psychotherapists or psychiatrists.

The trouble is that this elephant is actually like a wizard that can conceal itself from us very effectively. Like Harry Potter, it wears a cloak of invisibility. This elephantine wizard *Id* can fool us anytime it wants. Our *Id* has such an amazing array of tricks and spells that even the most brilliant *Ego* is left bamboozled by it. This makes hunting it out one of the most important, exciting and sometimes frustrating adventures of them all.

The reason it is so important to understand this *Id* is simple. How we deal with the *Id* lies at the heart of our success, our happiness and our peace of mind. It seems we cannot achieve happiness or success if we just walk around the place denying the existence of elephants. As Eric Berne put it:

"No matter how clever a man is with other people and with the things around him, he will not find contentment unless he can deal with his own Id as well. In the end it is not the ability to charm women or to make money that leads to happiness, but the ability to make peace in one's own mind."

To be successful in life we must master *The Self*. To do this we must master *The Id*. This is not something that is a luxury in life; it is a basic necessity. Mastering the *id* lies at the heart of all success and happiness. Nor is it something that is important only for the mentally ill. We all need to learn how to exert control over our lives and take charge of our destiny, no matter what genetic or postcode lottery we may have been born into and grown up with.

This is where the psychological disciplines come into their own and why they have so much to teach us...

7

UNDERSTANDING PSYCHOTHERAPY

"Psychotherapists can use an archeological or an architectural approach..."

The last 200 years of psychiatry, psychoanalysis and psychotherapy can be summed up as using either an **archeological** or an **architectural** approach, or some combination of the two.

THE ARCHEOLOGICAL APPROACH

Those approaches that adhere to *the archeological philosophy* tend to do a lot of historical digging around into an individual's past. They look for evidence of ancient dysfunctional behaviour and archaic wounds. These approaches seek to find the prime cause of aberrant behaviour in the individual's early childhood and to make therapeutic interventions that are designed to influence this.

They deal largely with changing the unconscious mind; *the Id.*

In order to reach far back in time these therapists often use hypnosis, free association or the attachment of a deeply therapeutic relationship, sometimes built up over years. These techniques are all used to "lift the veil" of the psyche's protective wall of denial and memory suppression.

This approach tends to rely heavily on the work of Freud and psychoanalysis. Transactional Analysis is firmly rooted in these archeological traditions, sharing the same origins. Most of the research into the unconscious supports the importance of these early years in the development of our personality.

THE ARCHITECTURAL APPROACH

Those approaches that adhere to what I call *the architectural philosophy* tend to do a lot of psychological rebuilding in the "here and now." They do this to repair any dysfunctional behaviour in the present. Their main purpose is to avoid immediate psychological collapse. They do not pay so much attention to historical causation. Their main focus is to build new behaviours that enable the person to function successfully, right now.

They deal largely with changing the conscious mind.

This approach tends to use cognitive and behavioural techniques aimed at stabilising the person's life in the present. Transactional Analysis also fits into this category, with its emphasis on the "here and now reality" and on strengthening the conscious mind of the person concerned. This same "Adult strengthening" approach can be found in a whole range of cognitive and behavioural approaches to psychotherapy.

It is also true to say that:

Archeological therapy, if successful, will have a "bottom up" impact on the here and now architecture of the conscious mind.

Architectural therapy, if successful, will have a "top down" impact on the archeological wounds in the unconscious.

THE SOMATIC APPROACH

Another approach that deserves mention here combines both archeological and architectural elements. This involves therapists who subscribe to what I call *the somatic philosophy*. Soma is Greek for "the body." These approaches tend to engage the body and the breath a great deal. They tend to look for the physical signs of dysfunction and to unpack and re-route such energetic disturbances to the somatic self. Such somatic approaches can be broadly divided into either Body Psychotherapy or Bodywork.

Body Psychotherapists aim to explore the awareness of bodily sensations and feelings and give voice to them. This somatic approach enables us to access the hidden and long forgotten primal causes of dysfunction that lie in our unconscious. The body holds a great deal of our suppressed material in its soft tissues. In this sense it could be said to be an *archeological approach*.

Bodywork aims to affect the immediate here and now conscious reality by reducing tension, increasing freedom of movement and ease of breathing. It could therefore be said to be an *architectural approach* that seeks new freedoms in the "here and now."

Either approach can have an impact on both the architectural and archeological levels.

It is quite common for archeological shifts to happen completely naturally and effortlessly in the course of a Bodywork session. This is especially true where simple touch is the primary focus, as in Massage. The cathartic release of suppressed unconscious materials lurking deep in the tissues of the body is a regular occurrence for those bodyworkers who work primarily with touch in total silence.

Touch does that. This is because it stimulates the part of the human psyche that continually seeks homeostasis. In the presence of simple healing touch, the client is free to release and dissolve ancient patterns of tension and belief however and whenever they are ready to do so. Sometimes this may happen with convulsive sobbing and sometimes with a single sigh. Sometimes it happens at the first session, and sometimes at the hundredth.

The evidence that such Bodywork is also an archeological approach lies in the way that a person turns their life around without a "psychological word" being spoken. It is often forgotten that Freud himself began with Massage and Bodywork because of its hypnotic and cathartic effect. Having regular

Massage where deep and healing touch is the sole focus of the treatment is actually one of the most effective ways to release archaic tensions and bring the unconscious into harmony with the conscious.

Whatever approach we favour; architectural, archeological or somatic, we are going to need an accurate map that will help us navigate through this territory of the human mind…

8

A MAP TO NAVIGATE WITH

"T.A. is a system based on solid psychiatric and psychoanalytical clinical traditions"

FRAN

To navigate our way through the murky waters of the human psyche we are going to use the approach of Transactional Analysis. There are four reasons for this:

Firstly, it is a system based firmly on solid psychiatric and psychoanalytical clinical traditions. This means it addresses the archeological levels of the psyche.

Secondly, it is based on changing our observable "here and now" behaviour, which means it also deals with the architectural and behavioural aspects of the psyche.

Thirdly, because of the observable nature of this approach you can make your own assessment of its accuracy without needing to take my word for it.

Fourthly, such a simple and down to earth approach means we can avoid wasting our time on unnecessary theories, speculations or interpretations.

Einstein is attributed with saying: "*If you can't explain it to a six year old, then you don't understand it yourself.*" It would seem that Eric Berne is one of only a handful of psychological professionals who understood this axiom. Berne's knowledge of both psychiatry and psychoanalysis was profound. His determination to make complex ideas accessible to us all was clear from the title of his very first book "*A Layman's Guide to Psychiatry and Psychoanalysis.*"

As we shall see later on in this book, it was Berne's mission to make psychoanalysis and psychiatry more practical and more understandable to the public. In this he succeeded beyond even his wildest dreams. That his ideas actually worked can be seen in the fact that more than forty years after his death, Transactional Analysis Psychotherapy continues to grow from strength to strength with over ten thousand psychotherapists using his ideas in their clinical practice, all around the world.

Berne's ideas have shaped the direction of psychological thinking. Many of his concepts have entered the mainstream of psychotherapy, often without proper attribution. His introduction of therapeutic contracts and his description of ego states predate all of their subsequent appearance in mainstream psychological literature. One of the reasons for this immense success is Berne's ability to make complex ideas simple. His definitions of strokes and scripts and games cut to the quick of so much long winded theory. He did this in a highly practical manner. That is the main reason for using Transactional Analysis as our map. It can help us to navigate our way through just what *being human* really means in a practical way. It makes complex ideas simple. Above all, it is applicable and practical.

It is almost impossible to learn about the ego states, as we shall do, without experiencing a new awareness and control over our behaviour, thoughts and feelings. Berne's unique model of the ego states enables us to understand and redirect many of the destructive thoughts and impulses that we use to sabotage our lives.

Knowledge is power, and the power of this knowledge belongs to everyone, not just psychotherapists or psychological professionals. Prometheus stole into the caves of the gods and returned with the gift of fire. Eric Berne stole into the caves of 200 years of psychoanalysis and returned with the gift of the ego states. I have been teaching this material to hundreds of students for almost twenty years and find it to be as powerful as any therapy. Watching and hearing the changes that my students make to their lives from the information contained in the next chapter alone, inspires me to keep sharing it with as many people as I can.

Education does that, it transforms us. Education is the most powerful therapy of them all.

By learning about ego states, we can learn how to shift the cathexis of our mental energy away from the destructive and habitual aspects of our psyche into the parts of us that are more effective. This is one definition of healing: to simply shift our mental energy from damaging and sabotaging areas into healthy and successful parts of the mind.

One of the most well tried and proven ways to do this is with Berne's ego state model...

9

THE THREE EGO STATES

"This model summarises over 200 years of psychological literature in just 3 seconds."

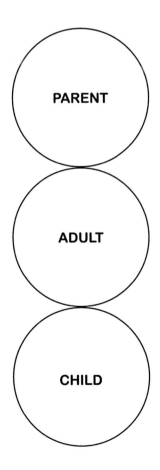

PARENT

ADULT

CHILD

To convey how the human mind manages our unconscious forces, Eric Berne came up with this map of our psyche. Other maps exist and other maps may be useful, but this is the map that we will be using throughout this book, and the *Psychology of Change* series. It has a *massive* proven track record in the treatment room, the classroom, in business and politics. By simply teaching this model, Transactional Analysts are able to give people real and effective control over how we express our unconscious urges. Put bluntly, it works.

Berne's map of the Parent, Adult and Child ego states is still one of the most stunning tools used by psychotherapists, trainers and business leaders to this day. Anyone who wishes to understand how human beings work will find this model to be highly effective. As with $E=MC^2$, we should not let its simplicity fool us.

This model not only summarises over 200 years of psychological literature in about 3 seconds, it also brings a new *observable* clarity to understanding human behaviour. It has helped millions of people take charge of their behaviour, thereby getting better results in their lives. This simple map explains human behaviour by what is observable. We call this *phenomenology*. We look at the observable *phenomenon* of human behaviour. There is no speculation involved. This was a radical departure from the psychoanalytical theory of Berne's day.

THREE DIFFERENT VOICES

Berne identified three patterns of human energy and behaviour. It's as if we all have three different voices inside our heads. We have a *Parent voice*, an *Adult voice* and a *Child voice*. Berne simply called them Parent, Adult and Child for shorthand, using a capital letter to distinguish them from an actual child, adult or parent. This is the system used in this book.

Each of these three "voices" represents a coherent pattern of thinking, feeling and behaving. Energy moves between all three. If it moves freely and easily whenever appropriate, then we say a person is healthy. If it gets stuck, then we call them sick.

We say we "cathect our Adult" when our energy is focused on a particular set of feelings, thoughts and behaviours that deal with the "here and now" reality of life. We might call this the problem solving voice.

We say that we "cathect our Parent" when our energy is focused on a set of feelings, thoughts and behaviours that resemble actual teachers or parents that influenced us in our past. We might call this the moral and ethical voice. We have actually stored the tone of voice and behaviours of specific people firmly in our memories. Most of us can hear the voices of our significant teachers inside our heads. The most uncomfortable example of this is when we catch ourselves saying exactly the same phrases to our children as our own parents used with us.

We "cathect our Child" when our energy is focused on a set of feelings, thoughts and behaviours that resemble how we actually behaved as children. We might call this the creative and emotional voice. We have stored experiences from our childhood as memories, right down to how we twiddled our hair in our fingers. Sometimes we notice that our voice takes on a more childish sound, and sometimes we wonder why we behaved in such a child-like way.

As we look at each of these ego states in more detail, you will see ALL human behaviour identified...

THE PARENT

This part of our psyche constitutes the observable behaviours, thoughts and feelings that we have internalised and reproduced from all the significant parental figures in our lives. This behaviour is therefore "borrowed" from others and is based on the past. This includes many of our moral and ethical views and beliefs. Berne called it "borrowed" because we literally store the mannerism and tones of voice in which significant people communicated these behaviours to us in the past. We can access our own versions of these behaviours whenever we need to. That is how we recognise them, because they actually resemble significant people in our lives.

This Parent contains many of our cultural traditions, handed down from one generation to another. The Parent is what the baby got from intense observation, copying and absorption of the important figures in its life. Whenever we cross the road or direct others in any way we are probably utilising our Parent. When we are discerning the right moral course of action for ourselves or others, we are listening to this voice. When a person starts wagging their finger at you, it is highly likely that they are "in their Parent." It is the part of us which takes into consideration the needs of others and our community. So here's what can go wrong with our Parent:

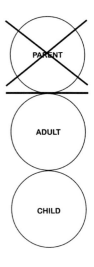

DISSOCIATION: *This means that a person has NO PARENT at all. Life is very chaotic without the Parent. Sociopaths and murderers either lack a functional Parent, or have dissociated from it entirely. They have no morality or respect for other people. We draw this extreme disconnection with a line separating the Parent from the other ego states. We draw a cross through the Parent to indicate its decommissioning. Therapeutically, the aim is to use the Adult to "rebuild a healthy Parent." This may involve learning the rules and morals of society from scratch (Architectural approach).*

CONTAMINATION: If life is run excessively from the Parent, we are likely to become overly caring or critical of others. Instead of being excited about something, we try and take care of someone or we start moralising. This inappropriate Parent behaviour indicates that the Parent is "contaminating" our Adult. It does not happen all the time but the more it happens, the greater the contamination. We draw it with the Parent covering some of the Adult (shaded area). Therapeutically we aim to strengthen and "decontaminate" the Adult from these persistent Parent prejudices (Architectural approach).

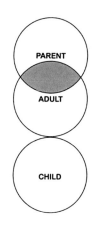

EXCLUSION: If life is run exclusively from the Parent, then we become physically and mentally rigid and "old before our time." This is THE ONLY BEHAVIOUR that we see. People in this condition end up sitting in pubs or cafés lamenting "the good old days" and criticising the replacement of real music by rap. We see them continually sermonising and laying down moral "shoulds" and "oughts." The joy and excitement of the Child is completely suppressed, making life a tad tedious during the day and at night times, frigid. If the Parent is "running the show" like this, then we draw this EXCLUDING Parent with a reinforced and darkened circle to indicate its dominance. Therapeutically we aim to first work with the Adult (Architectural approach) and then increase the flow of energy to the other ego states (Archeological approach).

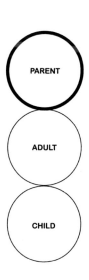

THE CHILD

The Child consists of the observable behaviours, thoughts and feelings that we have internalised from our actual experiences as children. They are exact replicas of behaviours we used as children. If you watch family members greeting each other after a long time apart, you are likely to see an example of this excitable "child-like" behaviour. At such times we revert to a time when it was OK to express emotion. Partners are often shocked when they see their "other half" suddenly behaving in a childlike way with their actual parents.

Like the Parent, this Child voice is based on the past. Instead of borrowing it from another person, we have actually experienced it ourselves. This is why it is full of raw emotion and energy. When we are having fun or expressing our emotions or being particularly selfish, we are "in our Child." This is the creative and expressive part of our psyche and life would be very tedious without it. Here are some of the things that can go wrong with the Child.

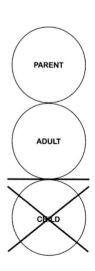

DISSOCIATION: *People who find it hard to be excited or joyful or creative at all have dissociated from their Child. These are joyless beings. An extreme example is the catatonic who has severed himself from the Child entirely and has no energy for life or people at all. We draw this with a line severing it from the other ego states, and a cross to indicate which ego state is no longer active. Therapeutically, the first step is to strengthen the Adult in order to "reclaim the Child" once again (Architectural approach).*

CONTAMINATION: *If life is run a great deal from the Child, then there may be a lot of fun and drama. However, these people may struggle to form secure and long lasting relationships. They are unlikely to succeed financially and materially in life. They will have a lot of friends who are creative and all very "exciting" but they still rely on the grown up government to provide them with unemployment benefit or sick pay. Long term security and pleasure is sacrificed for the immediate short term "highs" of the present. Drug and alcohol addictions are the favourite pastimes of the Child. This is because of the immediacy and ease with which we can "feel good" when we use them. We draw it with the shaded area representing the overpowering of Adult by Child. Therapeutically, the aim is to strengthen and "decontaminate" the Adult (Architectural approach).*

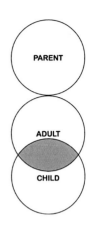

EXCLUSION: *When the Child is "running the show" entirely, we tend to witness immoral and antisocial behaviour. The self centred behaviour of music "Divas" would be a good example of this personality. This is because the Child is little concerned with the needs of others. If this happens and there is no remorse, then what we have is an EXCLUDING CHILD which is drawn in this way, with a reinforced circle. Idi Amin would be a good example of an excluding Child personality. Therapeutically, the aim is to first energise the Adult (Architectural) and then work with the Child to allow energy to flow to the other ego states (Archeological approach).*

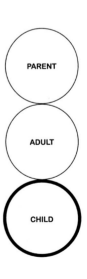

THE ADULT

The Adult consists of the part of us that deals appropriately with the "here and now." This is the problem solving part of the human psyche and the part which attempts to make things work in the real world. It is the part of us that fixes the car, regardless of our Parent thinking "cars should not break down," or our Child wishing that we owned "a better car."

The Adult is the part of us that balances our own personal and sometimes selfish needs, often emanating from the Child, with the correct moral behaviour needed by society, often emanating from our Parent. It is the Adult that decides which particular course of action to take that will give us the best possible outcome in the real world.

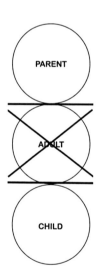

DISSOCIATION: People with psychosis, many of whom live in mental wards, have severed themselves off from their Adult completely. This is how they can "flip" from a vicious and critical Parent voice straight into a highly emotional Child voice. This is one way to understand manic and schizophrenic behaviour. They literally hear Parent and Child voices and think they are real. Such behaviour may also contain moments of lucidity (Adult) which are immediately forgotten when energy is locked back in the other states. We draw it as being severed from the other ego states and with a cross to signify its decommissioning. Therapeutically, the aim is to connect all three ego states back together again, so that each is aware of the other. We do this by focusing on rebuilding the Adult (Architectural approach).

CONTAMINATION: *Because much of our successful behaviour stems from the Adult, we do not regard a contaminating Adult as a "bad thing." Because the Adult is reality based, there can be no contamination of the Parent or Child by the Adult that is inappropriate. What we see mostly is a WEAK ADULT which results in a double contamination by both the Parent and Child ego states. We draw it with the shaded areas indicating these contaminations. Therapeutically we aim to strengthen the Adult so it can exert more control and "push" the Parent and Child voices out (Architectural approach).*

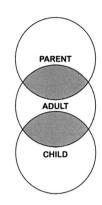

EXCLUSION: *If life is run continually from the Adult, then we are unable to connect with either the joy and energy of the Child or the wisdom and morality of the Parent. When you meet someone in this state, it is a bit like talking to a machine. Everything is reduced to its logical and rational component. It is the scientist or the accountant, without feelings or morality. Such conversations tend to be tedious or scary because of the lack of either emotion or morality. This is called an EXCLUDING Adult and we draw it with a reinforced circle to indicate such a "fixed" way of living; purely in the Adult ego state. Therapeutically we aim to bring awareness of the other ego states to the Adult so that energy flows to both the Parent and Child (Archeological approach).*

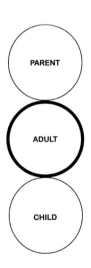

So just how does our energy flow between these different ego states and what can we do if we want to change from one to the other?

10

THE FLOW OF
ENERGY - Cathexis

"Energy flows continuously between Parent, Adult and Child in a healthy individual."

BOUND ...FREE AND POTENTIAL ENERGY

Energy flows continuously between Parent, Adult and Child in a healthy individual. This movement of energy is called cathexis. This can only happen if enough energy is able to move around as *"Free Energy."* This means that when out with friends, we can *cathect* our Child and have fun and excitement. It also means that when a friend falls over and breaks his leg, we can immediately get him help, by moving energy to our problem-solving Adult. When we are tired after such an eventful evening, we can then use our free energy to *cathect* our wise Parent and go to bed at a sensible time so we have a good day tomorrow.

If we are struggling with life then we may get stuck in certain behaviours over and over again. This is because our energy has become locked, or *"Bound."* This means when we go out with our friends we may tell them what they "should do" from a bossy and critical Parent voice, when everyone else just wants to have fun. Alternatively, it could mean that when we are tired we ignore our body's needs and take stimulants to keep going. This is because our energy is bound in our Child ego state, which doesn't want to stop having fun. If a sad friend just needs a warm hug and a caring ear, it could mean that our Adult unhelpfully goes and suggests thirty five different ways to fix it. This is because our energy is *"bound"* in the Adult.

As well as *"Free"* and *"Bound"* energy, there is also a third package of energy, called *"Potential Energy."* This is energy that appears *"Bound"* at first, but proves susceptible to movement when prodded by ourselves, a therapist, or by just reading a good book about being human. You see, it was only *pretending* to be bound.

So we have three types of psychic energy:

1. We have energy that is **"free."** This moves across all three ego states effortlessly, under our direction.

2. We have energy that is **"bound"** and appears fixed in a certain ego state. It is very hard to get this energy to move anywhere.

3. We have **"potential"** energy that appears at first to be "bound" in one ego state but which can move to another place, given the right encouragement.

People with lots of free energy generally don't need much help.

People with too much bound energy cannot easily be helped.

People who have lots of potential energy can be helped a great deal.

This is how we change; either by directing our *Free Energy* to a different state, or by stimulating *Potential Energy* to move to a different state. It should also be pointed out that even when energy appears to have been *Bound* in a particular ego state for many years, psychotherapy has shown it can "unbind" this locked up energy and turn it into potential energy, thus enabling us to change.

The simple technique to use with each difficult situation you find yourself in, is to ask yourself what your "moral," "caring" or "critical" Parent voice would say. These are the three most likely expressions of your Parent voice. Then you ask yourself what your "creative,""rebellious" or "adapted" Child would say. These are the three most likely expressions of your Child voice. Finally you ask yourself what your "problem solving" and "reality based" Adult would say. That way, you can access all the available options at your disposal and then simply choose where to put your energy. This is how you direct your free energy and stimulate potential energy to move where you want it to go. This will do it, most of the time, for being in charge of your life in an effective and successful way.

If we don't identify and then take charge of where our energy is operating from, then we end up in repetitive and dysfunctional behaviours. These dysfunctional behaviours were called *Games* by Eric Berne. This is how society allows us to release our destructive urges. He believed that by focusing more energy into our Adult, *"playing games and playing through one's script are optional."* Regarding games, he believed that: *"… a strong Adult can renounce these in favour of gratifying reality experiences."* This is one of the cornerstones of Transactional Analysis; that every human being has a functional Adult and can transform destructive games into meaningful encounters.

This means that we can all *choose* our behaviours. The example on the next page shows how this simple awareness of our three ego states and which we choose to cathect, can help us to succeed in life on a moment to moment basis:

CHOOSING WHICH EGO STATE TO CATHECT

It was 11am on a Sunday morning and I was travelling from Oxford to Manchester by train. I was having a very peaceful journey, doing some writing. Then we arrived at the NEC station outside Birmingham, and our carriage was invaded by a group of boisterous middle aged ladies from Stoke. They spread themselves out over the whole carriage and proceeded to converse with each other from one end of the carriage to the other in very loud voices. Their discussions of who was with whom and what went on last night left nothing to the imagination. Did I mention this was the silent carriage? Well it was. I noticed that I had three reactions to the situation:

1. *My Child wanted to stand up and start screaming at them to shut up and let me get on with my writing. "You are ruining my game!" would be the three year old version.*

2. *My Parent wanted to stand up and deliver a stern lecture about breaking the rules and being so antisocial. "Will you behave!" would be the shrill voice of this part of me.*

3. *My Adult looked around and saw that the reality was that I did not have a cat in hell's chance of controlling or changing the behaviour of these boisterous but quite hilarious Stoke ladies out to have a good time even at 11am on a Sunday morning.*

Consequently I decided to channel my indignant Parent energy and my annoyed Child energy into winning a new Adult challenge I set myself: to see if I could continue my writing and see the funny side of the situation. It was not easy to write with so much noise to distract me, but this "self challenge" worked. I enjoyed their riotous behaviour and got about 80% of my writing done. Even when one of these ladies sat right next to me and said "That must be hard to do, with all this noise about!" I cheerfully replied that I had three young children and could concentrate in the middle of a war zone. As a result of my ego state awareness, I quite enjoyed the challenge and "lived to fight another day."

Which cannot be said for the poor young railway employee who walked through the carriage selling sandwiches and hot drinks. He got three rows into the carriage before saying out loud "Excuse me ladies, but this is a quiet carriage!" Not a good move. By the time he got to the end of the carriage he had been verbally undressed every which way. "Hey Dot, I bet he wears them leopard skin underpants!" is just one of the more printable versions of the comments that were thrown at him. It was like watching a lamb going to the slaughter. He was bombarded with phone numbers, intimate questions and all sorts of outrageous and frankly, hilarious behaviour. For some reason, he never made the return trip to sell us more sandwiches.

The antisocial Child behaviour of these Stoke ladies had triggered a Parent response from the railway employee. With dire consequences.

In this example, success or failure depends only on
a) the knowledge of three different ego states,
and b) where we place our energy.

11

WHO'S RUNNING THE SHOW?

"Alcohol and drugs disable the Adult as does exhaustion and stress"

The real question for Berne was simply *"Who's running the show?"* Once alerted to the observable signs of our Parent, Adult and Child, it becomes possible to assess just where we and those around us spend most of our time. We discover some people have a Child "running the show" and others a Parent. We realise that these Child behaviours are always rebellious for some people, and for some they are always conformist or adaptive. We see that some Parent behaviours are always nurturing and for some, they are always critical and persecutory. Others seem to have a very tedious and moralising Parent.

With a little practice, it is possible to exert some creative control over the flow of energy from one state to another. This of course is done from our problem-solving Adult. This is the part of us that identifies the situation, the reality "out there" and decides which response is appropriate "from inside." Sometimes the Adult voice will respond with pure Adult behaviour, as in "here's how to solve this problem." At other times the Adult will select the right Parent voice to cathect as in "you poor thing, here let me give you a hug." At other times the Adult will select the right Child voice to cathect for a situation as in "Whoopee! This is fun!"

This is one definition of healthy and successful behaviour. Because the Adult is in charge, we can select the *appropriate* responses for each situation. We are discharging our creative and destructive urges in a way that society applauds. This is one side of the "success coin," the architectural side of it.

This drawing below gives us a picture of what architectural health really looks like within the psyche. The healthy and strong Adult ensures that we can access all the fun loving energy of the Child whenever we need that energy. It is the Adult that finds suitable ways in which to discharge the Creative and Destructive energies that need releasing from the Child. Instead of killing someone, we go for a long run. Instead of reaching out and handling a woman's breasts, we flirt verbally with her in a sophisticated discussion. This can sometimes be hard work for the Adult. This is why tiredness, illnesses and alcohol often accompany sabotaging behaviours. Alcohol and drugs disable the Adult as does exhaustion and stress.The Adult can also ensure that we access the moral integrity and wisdom of the Parent whenever we need to navigate through the more tricky moments of life. Thus the healthy Adult enables the safe and appropriate discharge of the *Creative* and *Destructive* energies that need releasing from the Parent.

Instead of physically attacking someone who "gets in the way" of our career, we resort to slanderous gossip about "that awful person." We behave in exactly the same way that a teacher who reduced us to tears in the past, once behaved. By cathecting this vicious Parent voice, we avoid being put in prison for murder.

Instead of expressing our inappropriate sexual attraction towards a new member of staff, we choose to displace the Child urge to suck her nipples by sucking excessive amounts of sweets. We employ a nurturing Parent figure who gave us sweeties when we were five. In this way we avoid getting the sack for sexual harassment.

Soap operas generally consist of removing much of the Adult in order to create the delightful dramas of the unrestrained Child and Parent ego states, necessary for exciting viewing. Most exciting literature and entertainment contains a moment when the main character did *not* cathect their Adult. Spotting this moment is one of the favourite pastimes of my students.

This knowledge of the ego states now means that we don't need a psychology degree to be effective or successful in life. We only need to pay attention to ourselves and to others. This is because:

All of human behaviour can be understood through simple observation of the degree to which someone is behaving from their Parent, Adult or Child.

Whilst ego states are an essential tool for unlocking the secrets of being human, there is another aspect that is equally significant. This concerns the deepest and most fundamental need of all human beings, namely our need for stimulus.

It is time to look at our stimulus hunger…

12

STIMULUS
HUNGER

"Folks need strokes."

"Folks need strokes" was the refrain of Transactional Analysis in the 1960's. What this means is actually quite profound. It means that, in order to survive in life we all need stimulation. A stroke is simply shorthand for "a unit of recognition." Although this can come in the form of physical touch, it includes any kind of recognition of your existence by another human being. This could be physical touch, a verbal connection or simply the raising of an eyebrow in visual recognition across a crowded room.

Recognition stimulates our nervous system. It is the main reason human beings live in communities, and do not live like hermits in isolated little tents all over the planet. We all need recognition from the rest of the human tribe. This need actually drives most of our behaviour.

The human organism will waste away and die without this recognition stimulus, even though the basics of food and water are present. The horrific stories of mass orphanages in central Europe provide all the evidence of this we could possibly ever need. Eric Berne put it succinctly when he stated that "if you are not stroked, then your spinal cord will shrivel up." There is plenty of research that shows that our I.Q. does not develop if we do not receive the stimulation necessary for the human organism to survive; the brain will simply not grow.

Our need for recognition strokes is one of the most powerful human survival drives. Stroking is what we do when we recognise and interact with each other. Without strokes, it seems our energy will simply wither away and die. This means that an understanding of strokes is perhaps even more important than our understanding of Parent, Adult and Child. The purpose of all human interaction is to gather strokes. This is because strokes are essential for our very survival. Berne identified four different types of strokes:

1. *Positive* strokes that are *unconditional* such as "I love you." These are strokes for who you are, regardless of what you do.

2. *Positive* strokes that are *conditional* such as "I love your cooking." These are strokes that are based around what you do.

3. *Negative* strokes that are *unconditional*, such as "I hate you." These are unpleasant strokes for who you are, regardless of what you might do.

4. *Negative* strokes that are *conditional*, such as "You are so clumsy." These are unpleasant strokes that are based around what you do.

They are all strokes and they all stimulate our spinal cord. They are as necessary for life as food, and possibly more so. It does not matter whether the transaction feels pleasant or nice, what matters is only that it is a *"unit of recognition."* The famous experiments of Harry Harlow showed that baby monkeys would approach a cloth "mummy" that had no food, rather than a wire "mummy" that provided food. The nurturing stimulus gained from the soft "mummy" was more important than food.

Our need for stimulation is one of the keys to understanding human behaviour.

The whole of human interaction can be understood in terms of our need for strokes. For example:

When a young child does not get enough recognition or stimulus from his parents for good behaviour, he will start to behave badly. If this gets him sufficient attention he will be

69

satisfied and repeat this behaviour whenever he needs more stimulus. However, if his bad behaviour is also ignored because his parents are "off their heads" on drugs, then he will escalate so that he starts to get into trouble with his teachers. If they simply keep putting him into detention or excluding him from school, he still gets no strokes. So then he escalates his behaviour even further and starts breaking into people's houses. This means he can now get his strokes from policemen chasing him and from all the dramas of the prison system when he gets caught. Whatever he thinks or says, he is driven by a need for strokes, which is why most criminals behave carelessly, as if they really do want to get caught.

Those cultures that excel in achievement give plenty of strokes to their children. The interesting thing is that they mostly give *negative* conditional strokes. Many successful cultures are renowned for telling their children that what they do is "not good enough." Even if they get a high grade, they are told they should have come top of the class. If they come top, they are told they should have scored 100%. These *negative* conditional strokes might be shocking to many "soft" westerners, but they prove their effectiveness in both educational success and high income levels in all studies of the subject. Their children are getting the same amount of spinal cord stimulation from such negative strokes as they would from positive strokes.

Interestingly, many such "tough" cultures often give their children an underlying unconditional stroke, through a belief in their innate superiority over other cultures. Their children must prove this superiority, or their parents will suffer shame. This drives their parents to give a lot of recognition regarding their academic work. This is in stark contrast to the *laissez faire* attitude of many "child centred" western parents who just want their children to be "happy."

Likewise, the more punishment we give to the badly behaved, the more strokes we give them *for behaving badly*. If we do not give them the negative strokes of "punishment" for early bad behaviour, we may end up having to give them "big punishments" like prison later on. Once we realise that the purpose of bad behaviour is spinal cord stimulation, we can stimulate our children in an informed and effective way. Whatever behaviour we stroke (regardless of negative or positive strokes) is the behaviour that will be repeated. For this reason we should always stroke the behaviour we want in others. It appears not to matter if we stroke them negatively or positively, hence the cartoon at the top of this chapter.

Any parent knows that if you give a child attention when they behave well, then they repeat this behaviour. It is just a bit strange to get our heads around the fact that a negative stroke will work as well as a positive one. Very often this is actually reversed in schools. The best behaved children in a classroom are often the most ignored. They get no strokes because they are "no trouble." To get strokes, they must learn to be naughty. It is the same with parenting. If we take for granted the things our children do well, they will have to find things to do that cause us to shout and scream at them. There is plenty of spinal cord stimulation in all that shouting and punishment. Creating that same "stroke energy" for good behaviour is a real challenge.

Conversely, if we remove strokes and just "shun" or exclude people, then we run the risk of driving them into more extreme behaviours in their desperation to get strokes. Ultimately, there is the danger of producing a "lone wolf" gunman on the prowl for one massive negative stroke pay off. So what must we do for people who behave badly?

If we give them negative "punishment" strokes for their bad behaviour, we are still rewarding them. Consequently, they will repeat their bad behaviour.

We need to give these people recognition strokes for what they are doing well, whether these strokes are negative or positive. The traditional boot camp works well for this very reason. Here, participants are shouted at and abused whilst training to achieve healthy behaviours. The problem here is that we must be around them a lot more in order to spot these moments. Those institutions that are successful in shifting behaviour from negative to positive outcomes are almost always intense.

The famous KIPP charter schools that are springing up all across America are a good example of the effectiveness of building such an intensive stroke economy. Founded by David Levine and Michael Feinberg in 1994, these schools require a strict adherence to a gruelling 12 hour school day with several hours of homework to be done additionally each night. They are the only academic institutions to repeatedly achieve such significant measurable successes across literacy and numeracy markers. Many of them are in poor and deprived neighbourhoods with class sizes as big as 35. It is not about resources, it is about their stroke economy.

The lack of such an intensive stroke economy geared towards successful behaviour is why the isolated, poor and disenfranchised so often resort to criminal behaviour. They are experiencing a lack of strokes from individuals and society and so must resort to getting stimulus from the police and prison system. To compound the problem, urban gang culture often provides a rich source of strokes. These gangs evolve simply to fill a stroke vacuum in their neighbourhoods. Organisations and institutions that provide communal recognition strokes for healthy and socially responsible behaviours are worth their weight in gold to any community and society. If we were really interested in solving crime, then this is what we would focus our resources on; supporting local organisations committed to rewarding healthy behaviour with strokes.

There is another problem around strokes. If we wish to understand and use strokes effectively, it is important to realise that the words alone do not do it. It is about energy. If you are genuinely pleased with a child's behaviour, then this must be conveyed non verbally with the same level of intensity that you express anger. We are talking about your non-verbal communication here. Matching the enormous energy of a negative stroke with an equally charged positive stroke is quite a challenge. To understand this, imagine shouting at the top of your voice, jumping up and down and waving your arms, every time you say "well done" to a child. That might just come close to the levels of intensity with which most negative strokes are given.

With young children the reward of safe and fun "tickling" for good behaviour would just about match the somatic shock of a shouted negative stroke. Many so called positive strokes are actually delivered in anodyne, pale and energy-less ways such as "Well done, darling." This is a damp squib stroke and is treated by children in the way it deserves. This is why so many children prefer the greater voltage of negative strokes; there is so much more spinal cord stimulation.

If your children behave badly, then check out the degree of physical energy or "voltage" that you are putting into your positive strokes when you are pleased with their good behaviour.

> *My own 15 year old son loves the highly physical sport of ice hockey. It doesn't get more physically exciting than speeding down an ice rink at 40 mph and smashing into another teenage boy! So this has become his stroke reward for completing his exam revision schedule each week. The physicality of ice hockey has now become his weekly stroke for good behaviour. He studies hard or he doesn't go to*

hockey. This is a positive stroke that is conditional upon his schoolwork. The result? This simple understanding of strokes resulted in a change of behaviour that meant he revises for over 14 hours a week. Prior to this he was averaging 2 hours a week, despite a lot of negative "nagging."

This demonstrates how our knowledge of strokes can have an immediate impact on our family and work life. Examine the intensity and voltage of your strokes. Think about this at the physical and energetic levels as well as at the verbal level. Words generally comprise about 20% of our actual communication with each other. The rest is made up of movement, tone of voice and energy.

So how does our need for strokes affect the way we structure our lives?

13

THE FIVE HUMAN INTERACTIONS

"How we structure our time is decided upon in our very early years"

It is our need for strokes that leads us to interact with other human beings. There are many different levels of human contact, each bringing with it a differing level of intensity of strokes for us. Berne called these activities "Time Structuring" because they define how we structure our day.

From the cold isolation of withdrawal to the warmth of intimacy, we see a progressively richer source of strokes. This increasing richness or voltage of strokes is also accompanied by a progressively greater risk of being hurt by another human being. The closer we let people get (because we need strokes), the more we risk them hurting us. This is the basic dilemma of living as a human being. How we resolve this dilemma defines our lives. The degree of contact we have with others is what constitutes our "stroke economy" and controls the way we structure our days.

Some people have a stroke economy that means they are forever interacting with people. These are the sociable types who spend lots of time in the company of other humans, in their daily work and at evenings and weekends. Others are so isolated that they could literally drop dead in their houses and no one would notice for weeks. Each will have a very different structure to their day, according to their stroke economy.

For the purposes of clarity, let us just suppose that our "stroke economy" requires the electrical stimulation of 750 kilowatts a day to our spinal cord for us to be content. This will help explain the main differences between these different categories of human interaction.

1. WITHDRAWAL

As this word suggests, the only strokes we can get from this behaviour is looking at ourselves in the mirror and talking to ourselves. We can say nice or nasty things to ourselves, but each "self transaction" carries a very low voltage for our spinal cord. For the purposes of this explanation, let us say each of these self transactions gives us just a small electrical charge of 1 kilowatt per transaction. They do not contribute much to our "stroke economy." This means we are likely to develop a very poor stroke economy.

With this behaviour, in order for our spinal cord not to shrivel up, we must stare into the mirror all day long. Like Snow White's stepmother, we must continually keep saying *"Mirror mirror on the wall, who is the fairest of them all..."* Like Narcissus, we are so brittle and fragile that we are too scared to truly love another or let another come close. We simply stare at our own reflection. Perhaps bad stuff happened when we were young, so the only interaction that we feel safe with is our own. We crave the security of our own reflection in every mirror that we pass. So enamoured of our own safe image are we, that we do not even feel the immensity of our loneliness.

This "self stroking" is one reason why people who live on their own are renowned for talking and muttering to themselves. After a few years of this however, the need for a good spinal cord jolt becomes so intense that we may do something really big. This is why withdrawal is also the breeding ground for the phenomenon of the "lone wolf" murderers and political extremists like Anders Behring Breivik, who devastated Norway on July 22, 2011 by killing so many young people. In terms of strokes, the recognition Breivik got was global. After several years of isolation he created a "strokefest" for himself to make up for the years of stroke starvation.

Strokes are at the centre of most human behaviours. This is why killers leave clues so they are found. If they are not found, they must keep committing more and more reckless murders until they are found. They only get strokes when found out. When children play hide and seek, they really want to be found. It's no fun otherwise. This suggests that the real purpose of crime and murder is more about getting strokes than any discharge of *Destructive Energy*. Such a discharge could be easily achieved without capture.

Withdrawal, though low in strokes and spinal cord stimulation is a zero risk strategy regarding human interaction. If you only had negative experiences of human intimacy and relationship in your early years, then any contact is likely to be traumatic. Although there are real dangers for your survival with withdrawal, it offers security and safety from what is perceived as a much bigger threat - human behaviour. At the extreme end of this, when we finally realise that our spinal cord is shrivelling up and we must interact, we may conclude that the only way we can survive is by killing people. For some people, humans all appear dangerous, so the only safe interaction they can actually conceive of is to kill as many of them as possible.

On a more positive note, withdrawal is an essential part of our balance in life. Having moments away from the stimulation of people is an important aspect of our human need for reflection, recharge and creativity. Having no withdrawal could be as dangerous as having too much.

2. RITUAL

These are extremely limited interactions with other human beings, and consist of the greeting we give the neighbour or the cashier in the supermarket. These interactions are ritualised and are expected to follow very rigid guidelines. When your neighbour says *"How are you?"* he is not expecting you to break down in tears and give a blow by blow account of your early childhood. What is expected is a well worked ritual of recognition exchange, that goes something like this:

"How are you?" your neighbour asks.
"Oh, can't grumble, what about you?" you reply.
"Same old, same old. Well, must be off - looks like rain..." your neighbour says, starting to walk off.
"And here I am without a brolly!" you shout back cheerfully, as you walk off in the opposite direction.

Each of these interactions carried both verbal and visual recognitions that meant you walked away with about 25 kilowatts of electrical charge to your spinal cords. Another 30 of these interactions and you will be content for the day. Once again, this behaviour is low on spinal cord stimulation and therefore risky for the organism. However it is a low risk strategy for the dangers and possible hurts that can occur from human relationships.

Another downside to *Ritual* is that it is very hard to change it into anything more intimate. Start talking at any length to the postman about your marital difficulties and you will witness his increasing discomfort. Go too far, and he will request a different patch.

The advantage of ritual over withdrawal is that at least there is some human contact and the spinal cord does receive a little *external charge* from this, every day. It can at least give the illusion of human interaction. For those who do a lot of withdrawal, these interactions can be highly significant. They can be the "high points" in each day. The lonely neighbour who is forever looking out from behind the curtains, waiting for the postman or window cleaner, is a classic example of such significance.

Ritual is actually the lifeblood of any community. It is often how local news is passed on and how human beings interact with large numbers of people in their community in a friendly and humane way. It oils the cogs of civilised society.

3. PASTIMES + ACTIVITIES

These are generally conversations and activities that you regularly share with other people, like singing in a choir or chatting with other parents at the school gates. There is a lot more flexibility around the rules of engagement in these transactions and they can go on for much longer than rituals. This means that you come away from your amateur dramatics group or your church committee meeting (where the *real drama* may have occurred) with over 100 kilowatts of electrical charge for your spinal cord. You can have many stimulating conversations along well worked themes, such as *"The good old days"* or *"My house / children / car are better than yours"* or simply having a good moan along the lines of *"Ain't it awful?"*

The way you engage in your pastime will tell others a great deal about you. You will learn a great deal more about the personality of your fellow singer in a choir than you will ever learn from the ritualised transactions with your local shopkeeper. This means that you can start to identify those people you feel safe enough with to progress to the next level of stroke intensity, *Games*.

Alternatively, you can remain at this "medium risk" level of contact and find lots of groups to fill up your life with. This is a much more stroke rich activity than ritual, say 100 kilowatt per group or experience. Pastimes enable us to spend long periods of time in a stroke rich environment, without having to progress to the more highly charged world of *Games*. I must have a hectic social schedule to fit in so many groups, but their main purpose is to avoid any further intimacy. The practice of rotating seats at dinner parties clearly demonstrates the need for this safe level of strokes.

4. GAMES

These might sometimes appear to be about activities, and look just like pastimes. However, they are really all about the relationship itself. This is a very intimate and stroke rich activity. A good game can give high kilowatt returns. Some games happen in a few seconds, whilst others can harvest strokes for years. Families are the best examples of environments where games can be played out for decades. With a good long term game we might reap our quota of 750 kilowatts a day as each stage of the game is experienced. Berne regarded all games as going through three basic recognisable stages:

The first stage is the opening "con" and "gimmick" stage, which explains why two people decide to "play." Player A might say to the other *"I have a nice pussy cat"* and player B might say *"I like stroking pussies."* So we have a game. What player A did not mention was the hidden second half of her sentence which goes *"and I like to make men pay dearly for stroking my pussy, thus relieving my outwardly directed Destructive energy."* What player B did not say was *"and I particularly like stroking the pussies of owners who will turn on me and make me feel bad, thus relieving my inwardly directed Destructive energy."* The main point at this stage is to locate a suitable partner for your particular game. There are a lot of *positive strokes* at this stage of the game, such as: *"What a nice pussy you have,"* and *"How nicely you stroke my pussy."*

The second stage of a game is called the "cross up" stage or "switch." This is where something "unexpected" happens. Player A remarks angrily *"I never said you could stroke my pussy that much! Just typical. Give a man an inch and he takes a mile."* and Player B feels all confused about the situation. This stage constitutes more negative strokes than positive ones. *"You stroked my pussy too hard!"* and *"I am rubbish at stroking pussies."* It is a necessary shift, because it then moves us into the third and final stage of every game.

The third stage is the "pay off." The pay off for A is the righteous indignation of *"Every time I let men stroke my pussy, they take advantage."* The "pay off" for B is the self loathing of *"look what a bad person I am - I can't even* *stroke someone's pussy properly."* The "pay off" normally ends the transactions with something like *"I have nothing more to say to you!"* This is because A has had plenty enough spinal cord stimulation for one day, or it allows B to start another game with another player. The strokes at this third stage are nearly all negative, but oh my, what excellent spinal cord stimulation!

The purpose of a game is to have dramatic and intense human interaction, without intimacy. Intimacy is considered too risky. This means that there must be a bad ending to each game so the relationship can either stop or it can start all over again right from the beginning. Either way, there is a limit to how close we can get to each other. There is an "intimacy ceiling" to all games.

So the purpose of a game is to have as much drama as possible without the dangers of intimacy. *Games* are the staple diet of soap operas. The main feature of a game is its bad ending. This means that one of the most common ways that we release both our creative and destructive energy is through playing *Games*.

5. INTIMACY

These are the genuinely satisfying relationships in life, where shared projects such as church or marriage or business are mutually enjoyed and genuine closeness and intimacy is maintained, sometimes over a lifetime. Because of their closeness, there is a much higher stimulation of the spinal cord. There is also a greater risk of being hurt by each other's comments or behaviour.

There is no need to break off these relationships as they are "game free" and are deeply satisfying. Meeting up for a meal once every six months can produce as much as a 10,000 kilowatt charge to the spinal cord, without the need for any trauma or drama.

What goes on is pure and simple; mutual human recognition.

The reason we revert to games, pastimes, activities, rituals or withdrawal rather than the fulfilment and happiness of intimacy, is because we carry an unconscious belief from our early years that "intimacy is dangerous." It is this unconscious belief that generally forbids us both the simplicity and the satisfaction of such relationships. Experience has taught us to fear both the creative and destructive urges of humans.

So what price is there in NOT having enough strokes in our stroke economy? If young, then we are more likely to be sick or even die. This is a well proven and observed phenomenon. If we seek outrageous ways to get strokes, then we may risk life and limb, and die. This is what happened to Houdini, amongst many others. Stunt men and people who do dangerous things for publicity would all fit into this category.

If Anders Breivik had recognised his difficulties with people and invested his time and energy in a therapy group instead of the isolation of making explosives and buying machine guns, then 77 young Norwegian people would still be alive and over 350 people would not be dealing with the physical and psychological trauma of those events. This is the price of both his lack of strokes and his lack of awareness of his need for strokes.

A therapy group could have enabled Breivik to learn how to get strokes through intimacy and how to release his *Destructive Energy* in more acceptable ways. Perhaps he could have chopped down lots of trees or taken a job with a demolition company. Spending time learning about his fear of intimacy and the reasons for this in a safe environment seems a small price to pay for over 400 lives. Understanding his low stroke economy and its relationship to destructive impulses would have transformed his life into something different. Learning to both accept his urges and understand their roots in his early life could have transformed his life and all those he hurt.

With genuinely intimate relationships in our life there is very little need for the energy draining drama of games. This means we have twice as much time and health available to succeed in whatever we wish to focus our life on. If career is what we focus on, then we excel. If health is our thing, then we amaze people with our fitness. If family and home is our priority, then people will remark on our happy family and lovely house. Thus one of the secrets to success lies in how we get our strokes. No one can succeed if their life is absorbed with intensely dramatic and destructive games. Nor can we succeed if we must isolate ourselves in withdrawal.

Intimacy is one of the major factors in building a successful and happy life. Only by dealing with these early beliefs about intimacy can we change the pattern of our human interaction. We need to create a rich source of strokes without destructive dramas. That is exactly what intimacy is; a rich source of strokes without time consuming and energy draining dramas.

With this information, it is possible to take a look at our lives and identify our own individual stroke economies. A common example is to be caught up in a lot of destructive games. Moving towards intimacy can create the time, energy and creativity we need to succeed more in our lives. To make such a change in our time structuring requires a lot of Adult energy.

This is because how we structure our time is decided upon in our very early years. If we start to move our stroke economy, we may find ourselves unconsciously sabotaging this. To understand more about this, we must first understand the concept of *Life Script*. It is this life script which sets up our stroke economy for the whole of our life. This is where we look at the second side of the "success coin," dealing with the *archeological* aspect of our psyche.

Up until now, we have been looking at what we can change by letting our Adult ego state run the show more than it has been. This *architectural* approach can often get us all the way to the success and happiness we are looking for. However, sometimes we find ourselves repeatedly sabotaging such attempts to behave in effective and successful ways. This is when we are hitting up against our unconscious life script.

This is why we need to know about the archaeological approach and how to make changes deeper down in the psyche.

14

LIFE SCRIPT

"That's how human beings are."

– Eric Berne

Berne maintained that we are living out our lives according to a life plan written by a three year old

The idea that we are all following a set script, written by ourselves before the age of five in response to circumstances that probably bear as much resemblance to our current life as nappies now resemble our trousers or skirt, is quite a horrifying thought.

Yet this is *exactly* what all those involved in the psychological sciences describe. They might do it in a variety of different ways but the consensus is clear; in our early years we lay down the template for our future life.

If we want to change that template we can do so, but we will have our work cut out. No matter how strange it might seem, Berne maintained that we are living out our lives according to a life plan written by a three year old. *"That's how human beings are"* is all he said when challenged about this idea by an interviewer. Here's what he wrote about this in his last book *What Do You Say After You Say Hello? (1972).*

> *"By the time he is six, our typical human being has left kindergarten and is pushed into the more competitive world of first grade....His mind is all wired up with his own ways of getting along, or at least of surviving, and **his life plan has already been made**." (p.97)*

Such early decision making about how life is, and how it will all work out in the end, is not done in isolation. Not one bit. The young child is engaged in specifically learning how to survive with these parents in this particular environment. The whole purpose of the life script is to make sense of the world we are living in at the age of three. This means that our life script was specifically designed to fit in with the world we were born into, and over which we had very little control.

Because we cannot control our environment at this age, to fit in we must change ourselves. We discover that, if we cannot change the "giant world" that we live in, we can change the world inside our heads. So we make up a story that "fits" and then we believe in that story passionately, as only a three year old can. We must write ourselves a story that makes sense of it all. This is why and how we each develop our own unique patterns of thoughts, feelings and behaviour. We each write our very own unique life script.

In writing this life script, the three year old is wrestling with exactly the same fundamental concerns about life and death that humans have wrestled with since the dawn of time. Life script is all about how we survive in this life, how we will live and how we will die. Berne put it thus:

> "The child is born free, but he soon learns different. During his first two years he is programmed mainly by his mother. This programme forms the original skeleton, or anlage, of his script, the "Primal Protocol" at first concerned with swallowing or being swallowed, and then when he gets teeth, with tearing or being torn. It is being a hammer or an anvil as Goethe put it, the most primitive versions of being a winner or a loser as seen in Greek myths and Primal rituals where children are devoured and the limbs of the poet lie scattered on the ground."

This is what lies at the heart of being human. Life script. It all comes down to the story that we tell ourselves. The tricky thing about all this is that much of what we are telling ourselves is unconscious. If we wish to improve our effectiveness in life, then we need to be able to have open access to this unconscious, and know how to "reprogram" it.

In his book *The Biology of Belief*, Dr. Bruce Lipton (2005) explains how the unconscious is like a tape player that just keeps on playing whatever story is recorded on it. He points out that no amount of "conscious" talking to the tape recorder will change anything that it plays. We must record a new tape if we want to hear a different story. How we do this will be addressed later on in the book.

Nor is it only psychologists and neurologists who are saying that we are all living out a life script which was "set" by ourselves at a very early age. Society has known about this observable phenomenon for a very long time...

15

A VERY OLD IDEA...

"The therapist of the future will concern himself solely with script"

– Eric Berne

Give me a child at seven and I will show you the MAN!

Versions of this famous saying are attributed to the Jesuits. Regardless of its roots, such a saying acknowledges the significance of the early years in forming a life script. Of course, early life script formation is not really a new idea. Society has always known the value of the first five years of life. This is why families gather around young children to celebrate their birth and their early years. We know that these are important times and everybody must help out.

Confronted by the somewhat tricky issue of continually needing new recruits for an organisation that advocated celibacy, the Jesuits famously discovered that if they could recruit children at an early age, they could then engender in them a life long commitment to their religious order. The fanaticism of the Jesuit order is a matter of historical record. Nor was the Catholic church alone in this practice of early indoctrination. If you give a young child over to any institution for early training and indoctrination, he is likely to belong to that institution forever. It is just how we are wired.

This can be seen in other organisations that require extremely high levels of loyalty and commitment. Hitler successfully indoctrinated young children with the *Hitler Jugend* in order to create intensely loyal cadres, many of whom were happy to "report" on the disloyal activities of their own parents. The Ottoman Turks trained young Christian boys to be the famed and fanatical *Janissaries*. Communist regimes still take young people into groups such as the *Komsomol*. In some countries it is still a common practice for childless adults to "purchase" young homeless children to train them to loyally look after them as their parents, in their old age.

Berne himself was always keen to point out that our early "life scripting" is not irrevocable. He was also crystal clear that it requires significant work to turn things around. After 35 years of clinical experience he summed up his findings by stating simply that people's lives were like a Shakespearean drama, often with three acts and a final scene of some considerable dramatic power. He called this final scene our "script pay off." Not only is script powerful, it is in the unconscious.

One of the major problems with our life script is that we do not know its full story until we are about to die. The last few years of a life have an uncomfortable habit of turning around the meaning of the whole story. How many of us would understand *Romeo and Juliet* if we had left the theatre before the last scene? Yet that is what psychotherapists are trying to do; blindly comprehend the direction and shape of a person's life script before the end of the drama.

Therapists, coaches and healers are generally doing their best to avert any harmful or tragic outcomes without any prior knowledge of just what is going to happen. It is rather like trying to guess the answer to a "Whodunnit?" mystery after reading the first page. We do not even know what crime has been committed. The importance of life script grew to become such a central part of Berne's thinking that towards the end of his life he said:

"Someday, someone is going to discover what human living is all about. I think the answer lies in script. The therapist of the future will concern himself solely with script."

This is why it is important to not only know about it, but to understand how we can change it. Strengthening and reinforcing our Adult awareness of our behaviour and directing our energy into healthy directions can work for improving a great deal of our lives. That is the power of the *architectural* approach.

The other side of the human success coin is learning how to rewrite our life script. This addresses the root cause of our sabotaging behaviour so we never have to deal with it again. That is "script cure." This is where we need the power of the *archeological* approach. This is what ensures we get the amazing power of our unconscious "on our side" when we want to make changes to our lives. Without this alliance of our unconscious mind, some changes are doomed to failure.

To make such archeological changes to our life script, we must understand exactly where our script is located...

16

THE LOCATION OF LIFE SCRIPT

"This is the part of our early child experiences where we made up our mind about life."

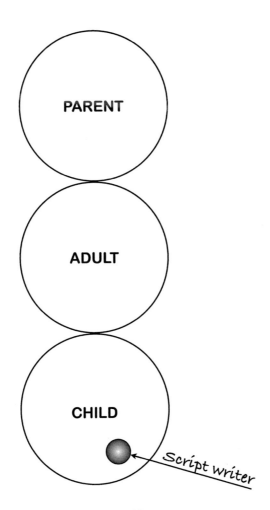

PARENT

ADULT

CHILD

Script writer

The picture above is a representation of how the human mind behaves and where the energy for our behaviour originates. This is not about its physical location in the brain. There is no Parent, Adult or Child segment of the brain. We are simply drawing a map that is helpful for making significant changes to our lives.

Actual research into the brain shows us that it largely works as a unit. To do something even as simple as moving my little finger almost every part of my brain is used. The brain works as a single and unified organism, much to the frustration of those of us who would prefer that separate bits of it did separate things. Nice and neat. In fact, one of the reasons that brain surgery actually works is because the brain has this ability to reroute itself in a myriad of different ways.

For Berne, the location of life script was very simple. We wrote it as a very young child. At the time, its main job was to get us out of fixes that we found ourselves in as effectively as possible. It is a template that lives in our Child. For our purposes we are going to call this part of the Child "The Scriptwriter." This is the part of our early child experiences where we made up our mind about certain aspects of life and then told ourselves a story that reinforced it.

Much of this was done pre-verbally at a time in our life when we were largely somatic beings. As we have seen, *Soma* is a Greek word that means body. Certainly the somatic nature of this part of our Child ego state would be true of what Berne called our "script anlage," or the primal script protocol. This was the early skeleton, the model we would use later on to actually build the more verbal Shakespearian details of our script around.

First comes a somatic feeling about life. Later on we find words to express this crudely. By the age of four we have identified a suitable story, most likely a fairy tale, that fits with our visceral and non-verbal experiences. By the age of seven we have written sophisticated Shakespearian dramas. As we grow older, we develop more and more sophisticated ways of living out this life script, leading us towards the final scene of the drama. Like helpless passengers in a raft we are headed towards the waterfall of our "script pay off." This is a final scene we actually decided for ourselves a long time ago. We may have no conscious idea what it is, but everything we do takes us in that direction, whether we like it or not.

The Scriptwriter is therefore a continual but invisible presence in deciding our everyday behaviour. This part of us is programmed to write each scene so that it fits in with each day's challenges and opportunities. Put bluntly, if we are confronted with a happy situation, but our life script is a tragic one, then we must find a way to turn the situation into a tragedy, or walk away. It is how we decide whether the glass is "half full" or "half empty." To use Berne's phraseology, it is why some choose to become the hammer in life, and others choose to be the anvil.

Although written in the Child, this script anlage is then adhered to by all three ego states. The Parent ego state may contain all sorts of functional wisdom and insight, but we somehow do not cathect that bit, just when we need it. Instead we access a part of our Parent that contains the necessary toxic messages to interpret each situation in such a way that our script is fulfilled. For example, I am out having fun with my mates, but I pick an argument with an old friend. At that moment I am accessing the same paranoid and argumentative behaviour that I saw my own father using when I was young. I turn a good situation into a bad one.

The Child may contain all sorts of healthy impulses and instincts for our happiness but just when we most need them, we cathect another part completely. In a moment of conflict, instead of resolving a difficult situation with a winning smile and a bit of fun, we become grumpy and disgruntled and so the situation escalates uncontrollably.

The Adult is perfectly able to select a different group of behaviours but just falls asleep at the critical moment. Our scriptwriter ensures that our toxic Parent and our grumpy Child become sufficiently energised that our Adult is completely smothered by their double contamination.

This role that our invisible scriptwriter plays is important to grasp. If we want to take greater charge of our lives then we need to update this outmoded scriptwriter who controls how we live. The stakes could be very high. As we saw in chapter three (Reality), we often find that our Scriptwriter has secretly been holding on to an escape plan that involves either suicide, homicide or insanity. Only if we know how to change our script can our most entrenched destructive behaviours be effectively changed once and for all.

To change script, we need to know more about it. We need to understand just how and why it formed in the first place...

17

HOW LIFE SCRIPT EVOLVED

"Life script is layer upon layer of physical, emotional, energetic and mental experiences."

The best way to understand how this all fits together is by following through one simple , but quite common, hypothetical life script narrative:

> At 3 days old Arthur was still struggling with feeding from the nipple and not surprisingly made up his mind that "Life is a struggle."
>
> Of course, he could not do this verbally. It started with a visceral FEELING comprised largely of hunger. This is an intense physical pain if Arthur's facial expressions are to be believed. This pain is also experienced with a fair amount of frustration and anger. Life is literally a struggle for Arthur. He does not have the cognitive function to understand any of the words that might be used to explain that mother is still learning to "let down" her milk. For Arthur, each minute of pain feels like an eternity.
>
> Later on, new sounds and movements would be added as he learned to mimic the frustrated groans and exasperated breathing of his mother, who is also in pain and frustrated. His mother had herself had a difficult time feeding after her own birth. She had no memory of this, of course. What she had noticed was a deep and visceral terror at the thought of breast feeding all through her pregnancy. She kept these terrors to herself. Arthur would find some satisfaction from mimicking his own mother's frustrated and angry movements.
>
> At about the age of two Arthur begins to understand certain phrases that sum up the basic family belief which goes something like "Life's a bitch and then you die." He soon starts to try out these "Destructive Energy" words and phrases, and

gets applauded by the rest of the family. He gets strokes for conforming to his family's belief system.

At about the age of four Arthur becomes attracted to the story of Cinderella. He finds a particular empathy for her poor treatment at the hands of the ugly sisters. He does not worry about the fact that she is a girl and he either conveniently forgets about the happy ending, or he simply does not believe it.

Arthur now has a fairy tale template which fits perfectly with his own script anlage or life belief. As he grows up he ensures that, even if life deals him a good hand, he stays in the cellar and makes it very hard for any "Prince" to actually find him. If this "Prince" of good fortune is persistent, he may eventually be forced to marry. In secret however, his script determines to return the world to its previously uncomfortable equilibrium at the earliest opportunity.

After every disconcerting brush with good fortune he finds a way to invite "the ugly sisters" of misfortune back into his life. As Arthur gets older he becomes increasingly bitter about "the hand that life has dealt him." He fails to see his part in any of it. Because of this bitterness he is passed over for promotion in his work and is always "the dogsbody." The pain in his life is only soothed by the all too temporary euphoria of alcohol.

Eventually this leads to him losing his job, his house and his health. Despite all the attempts of the "Prince like" social workers and care workers, his frozen body is found on a canal walkway one February morning next to a paper bag containing an empty methylated spirits bottle...

This all too real example demonstrates that our life script is in fact layer upon layer of physical, emotional, energetic and mental experiences. It also demonstrates that our life script resides in the Child, but it dominates all our thinking and behaving. It is a template for our Parent and our Adult as much as our Child. It can do this because it lives in our unconscious. It is not recognised and it is therefore not addressed. It just continues to plot its secret way to the final scene of our script drama.

This example also shows us that it is only when it finally coalesces into the shape of a fairy tale, that we begin to get a sophisticated handle on how to live it out for the rest of our lives. Going forward in our lives, we develop increasingly sophisticated ways to recreate this fairy tale story. Eventually we forget entirely that we were ever fascinated by this story.

The important point here is that our early script was written in a preverbal age where life was largely visual and somatic. At this age, whenever we were anxious or unhappy, we would express it as an upset tummy rather than in words. The stories we loved to hear were picture book stories, especially those told to us with a large amount of physical contact and cuddling. This combination of story, somatic experiences and vivid imagery probably helped us to form much of our life script. They became formative moments in the evolution of our archaic psyche. This was the language in which our life script was formed. Touch. Love. Safety. Physical cuddles. Vivid pictures. Fairy tales.

This somatic characteristic of early script is perhaps the most important thing to understand when it comes to working out how to _change_ our life script.

This language of our early scriptwriter is important. To reach back to the roots of any dysfunctional script behaviour, it is important to speak the language which this somatic scriptwriter part of our psyche will understand.

This alone may explain why life script has proven to be so resilient and difficult to change, in the face of so much "grown up" rational and verbal psychotherapy. The Child simply does not understand what is being said. This means we must understand the language of the stories that fascinated our three year old scriptwriter. This is the reason why fairy tales are so important. We need them to rewrite our life script.

So, to summarise, here are the two sides of the human "success coin":

ARCHITECTURAL: *We use our knowledge of the three ego states of Parent, Adult and Child and our stroke economy to take greater charge of our lives <u>right now</u>. We use this architectural approach to rebuild our lives in a healthy way, immediately from our Adult ego state.*

ARCHEOLOGICAL: *We use our knowledge of life scripts to redirect the flow and activity of our unconscious urges <u>in the long term</u>. We use this archeological approach to transform the original cause of our dysfunctional behaviour, so we do not need to use up so much Adult energy to function on a day to day level.*

So just how important is all of this? Let us take a look at what happens when we fail to master what being human is all about...

18

DANGEROUS

URGES

"This is how we
sabotage the things
we want in life."

This book started with the statement that "all life is energy." As we have seen, some of that energy is destructive and some is creative. Not handling or channelling the healthy release of both these energies can lead to problems. The build-up of suppressed unconscious energy can cause us to do stupid and dangerous things. This is why we sabotage the things we want in life.

Day to day, most of us are successfully limiting the damage that the negative aspects of our unconscious energy can have on us. We do this largely through our Adult ego state. Despite this, our suppressed unconscious urges are still roiling away like hot lava, deep in the psyche. They do this just below the crust of our conscious Adult control. If it were not for the reality controls of our Adult and our socially conscious Parent, the Child would act on impulse and explode these energies in a destructive way without any thought for either reality or the consequences.

On the day that I write this, there is news from Tampa, Florida of a retired policeman who was so enraged at the cinema by a man texting in the row in front, that he went outside to his car, picked up his gun and then returned and shot the man. The trailers were still running when he did this and the man involved had stopped texting by then. The featured film had not even started! It turned out that the dead man was a worried dad who was simply texting to see if his daughter was OK. The policeman's actions are a perfect example of pure destructive Child or Parent behaviour, untrammelled by any Adult. This retired policeman had been a model police officer. But after a lifetime spent suppressing his destructive urges in his job as a policeman and reliable public servant this man's unconscious urges finally got the better of him. State prosecutor Manny Garcia said of Reeves (the retired policeman): "He was a ticking time bomb that day — and he exploded."

It is only because of our Adult ego state that, on a moment to moment basis, we are able to choose socially acceptable behaviours, even when our feelings and impulses would take us down a different route. We might feel like shooting the man driving the car in front, but mostly we are able to suppress such impulses. We do this through the presence of both our moral and socially aware Parent ego state and our reality based and "consequence aware" Adult ego state. Whenever we choose to control and redirect our antisocial impulses and desires into socially acceptable behaviour, we are successfully proving ourselves stronger than our unconscious. For now…

However, this successful behaviour is not the same as releasing or rerouting the build up of negative destructive pressures in our unconscious. Only rewriting script does that. This series of books shows that by using fairy tales we are able to understand how to shift the very flow of our unconscious energy. We can re-route our unconscious energy, as well as control our lives from the Adult.

Adult control can simply drive our frustrated Mortido (destructive urges) and Libido (creative urges) energies ever deeper into our unconscious psyche. So instead of shooting people at cinemas who annoy us, or sleeping with whoever we fancy, we must release this suppressed energy in other ways. Sometimes we do this by murdering or having sex with people in our dreams. Remember that the unconscious does not know the difference between us imagining a thing and it actually happening. In this sense we relieve as much Mortido when we dream of killing as when we actually kill. We release as much Libido when we have sex in a dream as when we actually have sex in real life.

Either we must gain release of this pent up energy in our unconscious, or it must go somewhere. The first law of thermodynamics states that energy cannot be destroyed or created, only changed. So this energy cannot simply be suppressed or destroyed. It must release itself or it must change itself. If we do not release it in some way, then it must lodge in our joints as arthritis or it must start to constrict our blood vessels so we get high blood pressure. Alternatively, this energy may create illogical and neurotic fears in our mind, so that we get panic attacks for no apparent reason.

This build up of suppressed energy is dangerous and is exactly what we aim to avoid with a life script "rewrite." By rewriting our script in the archaic language of fairy tales, we can ensure that there is not such a build up of tension. We find new routes for both our suppressed destructive and creative urges. We create new and healthy channels for our energy. We create a new template, one that re-routes our energy and behaviour. We send a new message to our scriptwriter to write a different story. Life is all about the stories we tell ourselves.

With a script rewrite, instead of sabotaging our chances of promotion, we get promoted. There is no build up of Mortido because we are now getting satisfaction from our success. Frustration and rage find their new expression in achievement and success. Thus do we transform our deepest and most unconscious urges. This is my understanding of life script "cure."

This script cure means we do not have to exert so much Adult and Parent energy "controlling" these deep urges on a day to day basis. Consequently we have more energy available to succeed and to enjoy living life to the full. We are free to behave in a way that works with the world we now live in. In this way, we can see how success is intimately linked to our ability to direct and redirect our archaic and largely invisible life script.

Otherwise we all end up doing what we do, because of what happened to us in the first four years of our lives…

19

WHY WE ALL DO
WHAT WE DO...

"it is our life script
that determines
our success or
failure in life."

To succeed in life we must first understand why our lives don't always go to plan. We must understand why we so often seem to do exactly what we *don't* want to. To understand about success, we need to first understand how and why we *fail*. The psychological professionals deal with such failure and therefore have much to teach us. This book has summarised much of this knowledge by showing that we fail because:

> We are largely governed by invisible Destructive and Creative forces, of which we are barely aware.

> We are following a game plan written by a child of four, called our Script writer.

> This life script was designed for a completely different set of circumstances to the ones we find ourselves in, now.

> This life script is locked away in the inaccessible vaults of our unconscious.

> We sabotage genuine intimacy and healthy attachments with withdrawal, rituals, pastimes and games.

> We do not know how to harness the immense forces in our unconscious mind to work for us, rather than against us.

Fundamentally, we all do what we do because of a life script written before the age of seven. If we wish to master "being human" then it seems this is what we must master. Our life script controls the way we discharge our unconscious energy and it controls how we get strokes. It is our life script that determines the success with which we attach to others and the world. It is our life script that determines how happy we are and how many destructive games we play in our lives. Put bluntly, it is our life script that determines our success or failure in life. Only if we can master our life script can we be said to be fully free.

This is no small order. To change our life script is to alter the very template of our psyche. This template defines the way in which our *Creative and Destructive* energies are released from our unconscious into the world. If we change our life script then we change the way that this discharge occurs from the decisions of an ill-informed four year old to the decisions of an experienced and knowledgeable adult.

> **Taking charge of our life script and altering the way in which we release our unconscious urges is nothing less than The Holy Grail of all transformation, psychotherapy, mentoring and healing.**

We have seen how a great deal can be achieved by simply being more aware of the different voices inside our heads and choosing different responses. We can use our Adult ego state to do this. The moment we are aware of the destructive nature of these voices, we are not entirely controlled by them. Just by noticing them we have strengthened our Adult because this is the part of "us" that is now doing the "noticing."

Being human means we can use this noticing Adult to correct a great deal that does not work. This is the power of making *architectural* changes to our psyche. We do this by building and strengthening our reality based Adult. Often, this means that we simply "count to ten" and consider the outcomes and consequences of our behaviour *before* reacting. Most importantly, understanding this Adult voice means that we can make new decisions to remove the three escape hatches of suicide, homicide and insanity. Such decisions cut to the core of our destructive life scripts.

However, the real problem is that much of our life script lies *below* our conscious awareness. Much of it is, by definition, invisible to us. We don't notice it at all until after it has happened. How much of our self sabotaging behaviour could have been avoided "with hindsight"? How often do you wish you could have another chance? When confronted by repetitive destructive behaviours and *Games* that persist regardless of our best Adult efforts, then we are in the realms of our life script. Here we find that we need to adopt approaches that have an understanding of, and a respect for, the deeper *archeological* layers of the psyche.

Archeological approaches to change involve communicating directly with the unconscious and life script part of our psyche. Very often it is about creating a safe environment for the archaic Child part of us to even reveal itself to us. This is why historically, we have often needed the help of a skilled and trained professional to make a difference at this archeological level of the psyche. This is because normal "social" skills do not cut much ice here.

When we attempt to makes changes at this archeological level of the psyche, we are dealing with a part of us that likes to remain hidden and secret. We are dealing with our unconscious *Id*. It will not even reveal its name to us, so we hilariously just call it "*id.*" To access this part of the psyche we need to understand how to both understand and speak to this part of the psyche in its own language. We need to learn how we can make it our friend and ally. It is too powerful to simply be bullied by our conscious mind. Our Adult ego state is largely powerless when it comes to doing battle with such deep and tectonic forces within our psyche.

This is what I address in book two of this *Psychology of Change* series; how to understand and make friends with the vast forces of our unconscious, instead of having to fight against them all the time. Up until now, this has largely been the preserve of experts who have been specially trained in its arcane language. Psychoanalysts, psychiatrists and psychotherapists have to undergo years of rigorous training in order to even begin to "do battle" with the unconscious forces at play in the human psyche. Whole libraries have been filled with the reports of their journeys into this difficult and confusing land.

With The Fairy Tale Phenomenon, you can understand all that you need to know about the unconscious in just one book and you need no background in the psychological sciences.

NOTES FOR THE CURIOUS

FOREWORD

The aim here is to provide a simple, clear and practical summary of some very complex ideas.

With such a vast brief, much detail and many aspects of psychology and therapy have necessarily been omitted or brutally summarised. The purpose of this book is to clarify and simplify. Knowledge is power and too much detail can obfuscate that knowledge. This book is written to summarise the understanding of how human beings work after a life time of working in this field through Massage and psychotherapy. Like all knowledge, the more you know, the more you realise there is to know. For every page written, a hundred pages had to be left out. These notes are an attempt to guide readers further into some of those unwritten areas.

1. INTRODUCTION: "ALL LIFE IS ENERGY"

This energy only has one aim; to find balance.

The idea that we accumulate energy and then discharge it in order to find balance, with the second law of thermodynamics, can be found in the writings of Freud. His *Project for a Scientific Psychology* in 1895 describes psychology as the effect of the flow of energy through the brain. This concept that energy cannot be destroyed but must transform itself into something else, is at the heart of his work.

Again, it is all about discharge.

K.M. Colby described this concept of the accumulation of energy within the psyche and its need for discharge or release, in his classic *Energy and Structure in Psycho-analysis* (1955).

In the mind, we call this movement of energy cathexis.

Freud described *Cathexis* as an investment of mental energy in a person, an idea or an object. He described *Anti-cathexis* as how we block the socially unacceptable needs of the unconscious. This is the origin of his concept of *Repression*. In Transactional Analysis, the term *Cathexis* is used more specifically to describe the movement of psychic energy from one ego state to another. It is used colloquially as a verb, as in *"He then cathected his Adult ego state."* This is a usage of the word that is unique to Transactional Analysis. It was given particular emphasis by a whole branch of T.A. that called itself *The Cathexis School* (Schiff et al, 1975).

Since the time of Freud.

Freud called them the *life instinct* and the *death instinct*. The *life instinct (Libido)* relates to our basic need for survival, reproduction and pleasure. They include such things as the need for food, shelter, love and sex. Freud interpreted the psychological disorders of soldiers after the first world war as related to the *death instinct (Mortido)*. Self-destructive behaviour was just one expression of *the death instinct*. Any form of destructive behaviour, including warfare, would qualify as expressions of this *Mortido*.

2. CREATIVE AND DESTRUCTIVE ENERGY

We will call this *The Creative Principle*.

This is a simplification of what Freud called *Libido* which he also wrote about as the pleasure principle, in his *The Interpretation of Dreams* (1900). The ancient Greek philosopher Epicurus originated this idea. The nineteenth century radical philanthropist, Jeremy Bentham, also wrote: *"Nature has placed mankind under the governance of two sovereign masters, pain and pleasure."* The idea that human life is about seeking pleasure and avoiding pain is a part of the observable dualism that informs much psychological thinking to this day. Such a view is inherently superficial as it does not take into account the clear human predilection for suffering and pain as demonstrated by actual human behaviours like war, torture, sadism and masochism. This is what Freud addressed with his *Death Instinct*.

We will call this *The Destructive Principle*.

This is a simplification of what Freud called *The Death Instinct* and which others have described as *Thanatos*. Freud wrote about The Death Instinct in *"Beyond The Pleasure Principle"* in 1920. Melanie Klein broadened Thanatos to include a whole range of human behaviours such as envy, hate and aggression. This provides the all important link to Berne's *Games*. Whilst society applauds much Libido behaviour, it condemns the raw expression of murder and violence. This means that we have to find a way to discharge this destructive energy in a socially acceptable way. Playing destructive and damaging games, only a few of which end up in prison, was the solution that humanity came up with.

We learn to wait.

Freud used the concept of *The Reality Principle* to describe our capacity to *defer gratification* when reality does not allow the immediate gratification of our *Id* instincts. In infancy and early childhood we only seek immediate gratification. As we grow older, we develop this ability to defer gratification. Freud wrote that *"an ego thus educated has become 'reasonable'; it no longer lets itself be governed by the pleasure principle, but obeys the reality principle, which also, at bottom, seeks to obtain pleasure, but pleasure which is assured through taking account of reality, even though it is pleasure postponed and diminished."* (Sigmund Freud, *Introductory Lectures*, 1933)

3. REALITY

Identifying such escape hatches and helping clients close them is the first priority of any psychology professional.

It is inconceivable that we should concern ourselves with issues such as depression and anxiety before addressing such fundamental existential issues as going mad, killing ourselves or killing others. These "escape hatch" issues lie at the root of many dysfunctions and are often found to be their root cause. Very often people are shocked to discover that deep down, they hold such escape routes precious. For a brilliant article on this topic read Ian Stewart's *The Three Ways Out: Escape Hatches* (in Erskine 2010 chapter 6).

The issue of closing escape hatches is a big one. Stewart comes from the well proven classical tradition of Berne himself, where the emphasis is on strengthening the client's Adult so that he can effectively make a new decision about living. This can be done no matter what Parent messages or Child beliefs exist. It is an Adult decision, not an agreement from the client's Child to "please" the therapist's Parent.

Others would argue that a powerful and potent request from the therapist to close escape hatches may also operate as a permission "To Live." The insistence of the therapist's Parent that their client must stay alive and that they agree to do so from any or all of their ego states can act as a powerful permission. Such permissions can then become introjected by the client as new Parent messages which they can access at times of stress. This is important, as there may be times when the client's contaminated Adult may not be able to hold to the new decision to live, but the adapted Child remembers its agreement with the therapist and so stays safe. Here it is the relationship with the therapist that enables the client to stay safe. This is a temporary support as subsequent therapy is then aimed at doing whatever is necessary to strengthen the Adult and ensure that the client is free of such life threatening contaminations in the future.

If our early experiences in life...

The long term effects of early trauma on later life is the *Sine Qua Non* of most psychological research, theory and practice. The French neurologist Jean-Martin Charcot first wrote that psychological trauma was the origin of all instances of the mental illness known as hysteria. Freud was Charcot's student and developed this concept of original and early psychological trauma causing later dysfunction in life, throughout his career.

A more modern definition of this concept describes psychological trauma as: "An event in the subject's life, defined by its intensity, by the subject's *incapacity to respond adequately to it and by the upheaval and long-lasting effects that it brings about in the psychical organisation,"* Laplanche, J. and Pontalis, J.B. *The Language of Psycho-Analysis* (1967).

Berne himself simply likened this to a stack of pennies. If an early penny is "skew" then the whole pile is going to be off balance (Berne, 1961). This is just one example of Berne's pedagogic genius, using one simple everyday image to sum up several tomes of psychoanalytical theory.

Eric Berne called this unconscious part of us that is following a faulty map or picture of the world "a demon" (1972) p.134.

The psychiatrist Steve Peters has recently shot to fame with his work with top UK athletes, precisely by helping them to handle this demon of their unconscious. His ideas were summarised in his best selling book, *The Chimp Paradox*. Whether chimp or demon, both descriptions are attempts to express the instinctive and uncontrollable nature of our unconscious.

4. THE SELF AND OTHERS

We should regard our conscious mind...

This is a simplification of the psychoanalytical model where the unconscious *Id*, and *Superego* are both responsible for the internal forces of our *Libido* and *Mortido* urges. *The Ego* is the psychic organ that allows the expression of this according to *The Reality Principle* of the the external world. Freud saw *The Reality Principle* as the controlling force that civilised society as it controlled the lustful urges of *Libido* or *The Pleasure Principle*, Sigmund Freud, *On Metapsychology* (1991) p. 36.

So sometimes, we discharge our urges inwardly, instead of outwardly.

This section about the different ways in which we can direct our unconscious drives is a necessary simplification of the different ways in which we master *The Id*. Over the years, psychoanalysts have broken down the different ways we can deal with the forces of *Mortido* and *Libido* into six different pairs of behaviour options. To some extent, all six of these behaviours are in fact sublimations of our primal desire to either kill or procreate. Berne summarised these six different behaviours in *A Layman's Guide to Psychiatry and Psychoanalysis* (1968) p.75-84.

80% of all murders are committed by people acquainted to the victim.

Patrick Langan (et al) *Murder in Families* Bureau of Justice Statistics (1994). This study showed that 16% of murders are committed by close family members and 64% by acquaintances. A staggering 41% of all murders involved husbands and wives, as either murderer or victim. This statistic would be much higher if the parameters had included spouses who were recently divorced, which they did not. Alarmingly, 21% of all family murders involved parents killing their children. The report was compiled by the Justice Department's Bureau of Justice Statistics from an unprecedented examination of more than 8,000 homicides in 75 large urban counties. The cases were taken from statistics for just one year; 1988.

5. MASTERING UNCONSCIOUS URGES

Most modern research into the brain now shows that these same early years are precisely the time when we are forming most of our neural channels.

There is so much research that points in this direction, but two of the best known writers about this are Dan Siegal (1999) and Antonio Domasio (1994), though there are many others. It is fascinating how modern brain neurobiology is able to identify how our early development in life affects the very structure of our brains. The amazing work of Dr. Bruce Perry at the Child Trauma Academy deserves mention here. It is clear that modern science is now confirming many of the theories of Freud and psychoanalysis about the importance of our earliest years and early attachments in actual brain development.

6. THE EGO AND THE ID

This is why we often describe the forces of our conscious mind and our unconscious mind as being "at war" with each other.

For simplicity, I have subsumed the role of *The Superego* from psychoanalytical thinking into *The Id*. Classic psychoanalytical thinking defines the *Superego* as another aspect of our energy that is split off from the rest of *The Id*. This becomes a separate part of our unconscious mind that can punish *The Id* for gratifying its *Libido* and *Mortido* wishes in a way that it disapproves of. Both Id and Superego are in the unconscious.

Berne writes that *"In most emotional situations, decisions depend on the result of the conflict between the unconscious forces of the Superego and The Id. Once the decision has been made without the individual being aware of the real forces behind it, he takes upon himself the task of finding justifications for it and convincing himself and others that it has been made in accordance with the realities of the situation. This is called rationalisation."* A Layman's Guide to Psychiatry and Psychoanalysis, (1968) p.97. Modern research now supports Berne's idea that we act instinctively, based on the urges of our unconscious mind, and then construct a rational narrative afterwards. What is remarkable is that Berne was writing this *before* the advances in neurobiology provided evidence for it. For more information about this research read A. Domasio's *Descartes' Error: Emotion, Reason, and the Human Brain* (1994.)

"The reason that life is so difficult…."
Berne, E. *A Layman's Guide to Psychiatry and Psychoanalysis* (1968) p.75.

"No matter how clever a man is with other people…."
Berne, E. *A Layman's Guide to Psychiatry and Psychoanalysis* (1968) p.75.

7. UNDERSTANDING PSYCHOTHERAPY

The last 200 years of psychiatry, psychoanalysis and psychotherapy can be summed up as using either an archeological or an architectural approach, or some combination of the two.

This chapter is an attempt to simplify a field that warrants several libraries and buildings full of debating rooms. It should also be remembered that no two therapists ever work in exactly the same way. Each brings their own personal insights and history into the treatment room. For a more rounded introduction to the different approaches in psychotherapy see Stone, M. H. (1997) *Healing the Mind*; Szasz, T. (1997) *The Healing Word*; J. K. Zeig (Ed.) *The Evolution of Psychotherapy: The Third Conference*; and Viney, W. & King, D. B. (2003) *A History of Psychology.*

This approach is used by Body Psychotherapists...

Body Psychotherapy originates from Wilhelm Reich, a student and colleague of Freud. Reich developed the concept of 'character armour' to describe how human beings develop fixed and rigid postures and patterns of relating in order to protect themselves against emotional pain. These patterns reach all the way down into our biological mechanisms. Wilhelm Reich's pupils and followers developed particular aspects of his work further and diversified into a variety of modern schools of Body Psychotherapy, such as *Bioenergetics* (Alexander Lowen), *Radix* (Charles Kelly), *Core Energetics* (John Pierrakos), *Integrative Body Psychotherapy* (Jack Rosenberg), *Emotional Anatomy* (Stanley Keleman), *Biodynamic Psychology* (Gerda Boyesen), *Hakomi* (Ron Kurtz) and *Biosynthesis* (David Boadella), to name just a few of the more well known. For a fuller description, see *Body Psychotherapy - an Introduction* by Nick Totten (2003).

The release of suppressed materials lurking deep in the tissues of the body is a regular occurrence for those bodyworkers who work primarily with touch in total silence.

Unfortunately, many Massage traditions concentrate exclusively on fixing the structural and physical problems. However, we know that the human being is much more than just a physical body. It is the experience of hundreds of *NO HANDS*® Massage therapists worldwide that most structural imbalances will release in the presence of powerful touch. In such a touch rich environment, the client is allowed to release at *whatever level* the dysfunction may be held, physical, mental or even spiritual. Such releases are natural and happen without any artificial or therapeutic "push" by client or therapist. Whilst there is a great emphasis on silence and breath during the session itself, there is also a great emphasis on clear contracts *before* and on identifying observable outcomes *after* each session.

For more information about this approach go to *www.nohandsmassage.com*. You can also read my Massage novel *Mavis and I: A Journey of Personal Transformation* (2007) where such ideas are woven into the world's only novel entirely based inside the Massage treatment room. These ideas are further explored in my series of four articles entitled *The Psychotherapy of Massage: What Makes Us Human?* (*Massage Today*, Jan, 2014). These four articles can be viewed online at *www.massagetoday.com*.

8. A MAP TO NAVIGATE WITH

"It is based on changing our observable 'here and now' behaviours."
The many similarities between Transactional Analysis and the core principles of Cognitive Behavioural Therapy have been amply demonstrated by psychologist Joanna Beazley Richards, from the Wealdon Institute. *www.psychologytools.org/assets/files/TA_CBTA.pdf.*

"It was Berne's mission to make psychoanalysis and psychiatry more practical and more understandable to the public."
Berne's relationship with both psychiatry and psychoanalysis was complex. On the one hand he owed all his training and understanding of the human mind to these traditions. On the other hand, he regarded the increasing use of drug therapy in the psychiatric profession as disabling the all important Adult and psychoanalysis as unnecessarily long winded and drawn out. With Transactional Analysis, Berne empowered people to effect rapid changes in their behaviour on an architectural level. At the same time, his model enabled deep "psychoanalytical cure" at the archeological level, for those committed to restructuring their psyche. Transactional Analysis has proven itself remarkably successful in a comparative study by the late Theodore Novey, *Measuring the Effectiveness of Transactional Analysis; An International Study* in Transactional

Analysis Journal (V32, #1 Jan 2002). Transactional Analysis Psychotherapy continues to grow from strength to strength...

E.A.T.A. is the official European body for Transactional Analysis and the I.T.A.A. is the global body. Many countries have their own Transactional Analysis Associations. There is a South East Asia Association as well as Associations in Australia, New Zealand and South Africa. Here in the UK we have the United Kingdom Association for Transactional Analysis (UKATA). The Transactional Analysis community worldwide continues to demonstrate its organisational health with its continual willingness to accept, explore and embrace new approaches from a diversity of sources.

Many of Berne's concepts have entered the mainstream of psychotherapy, often without proper attribution.

The core concepts of Transactional Analysis lie at the base of much psychological writing, yet remain largely unacknowledged. This despite the fact that these concepts often predate such writings by as much as twenty or thirty years. A full summary of the core concepts of Transactional Analysis can be found on the ITAA web site *https://www.itaaworld.org/index.php/about-ta/ta-core-concepts*. Claude Steiner chaired a committee that comprehensively researched the numerous psychological concepts in use today that were predated by Transactional Analysis and these can be found at: *http://analyzingtransactions.blogspot.co.uk.*

9. THE THREE EGO STATES

This model not only summarises over 200 years of psychological literature...

The Ego State Model described in this chapter is largely the structural model. There is also a functional ego state model, which is only referred to in passing. Likewise, there have been many developments in Ego State Theory within Transactional Analysis since Berne's first book on this *Transactional Analysis in Psychotherapy* (1961). Perhaps the best exploration of this subject and of developments over the last fifty years, is *Ego States* edited by Charlotte Sills and Helena Hargaden (2003).

We look at the observable phenomenon of human behaviour.

This is the cornerstone of Berne's work and is where he parted company with the psychoanalytical approach of his day. The *Ego State Model* is based on the observable behaviours that resemble *actual* historic people or *actual* historical experiences. Berne's model was a development of the the the *Ego State Theory* of Paul Federn and the work of Erik Erikson.

With Berne's model, you witness the behaviours and hear the voices of *actual* parents and teachers (Parent). You also witness the exact behaviours we actually used as children (Child). Likewise, you witness people actually responding to the reality of the world around them in a functional way (Adult). This not only makes it a truly practical approach to therapy, but it also makes it a very exciting model to work with as it has a moment to moment reality, based on observable phenomena. It is quick and easy to learn and anyone can understand it.

This model can be found throughout his writing, but the clearest and simplest explanation of ego states can be found in his second book *Transactional Analysis in Psychotherapy* (1961). For a fuller description of Berne's life and contributions to psychotherapy, see *Eric Berne* by Ian Stewart (1992). The early roots of Transactional Analysis can be found in his early articles on the ego and intuition starting in 1949. See *Intuition and Ego States*, Berne, E. (ed. P McCormick, 1977).

10. THE FLOW OF ENERGY - Cathexis

For simplicity's sake, I have deviated slightly from Berne's description of energy. For Berne, "Unbound" energy was simply "Bound" energy that had been released. He used the image of a monkey sitting in a tree as "bound" and then when the monkey jumps or swings to another tree it becomes "Unbound" or "Free." I have given "Potential" energy this movable role for clarity. Apart from this minor deviation for the sole purpose of clarity, the rest of the material for this chapter is drawn from Berne's own writings in *Transactional Analysis in Psychotherapy* (1961).

"Playing games and playing through one's script are optional"
Berne (1961) p.260.

11. WHO'S RUNNING THE SHOW?

Fran's drawing of the ego states in this chapter is entirely my own design and neither he nor Berne can be blamed for any inaccuracies that it may represent to Transactional Analysis theory. It is my own visual representation of what healthy behaviour looks like in the face of self sabotaging urges. It is my own way of showing what is known as the "classical" approach to Transactional Analysis. One simple image can sometimes have as much impact as many pages of words. Strengthening the Adult ego state is the primary concern of all Transactional Analysts, before they ever launch into other, more complex archeological work with individuals.

12. STIMULUS HUNGER

The human organism will waste away and die without stimulus…
The wisdom in calling our fundamental human need for stimulus "stroke hunger" is borne out by the significance of actual touch to the early infant. The most stunning book about this relationship between the development of the brain and healthy human behaviour and actual physical stimulation, is by Ashley Montagu (1971). He writes: *"The evidence points unequivocally to the fact that no organism can survive very long without externally originating cutaneous stimulation."*

The horrific stories of mass orphanages in central Europe…
These stories were well documented on the B.B.C. by Kate McGeown in *What Happened to Romania's Orphans?* (8 July 2005) *Life in Ceausescu's Institutions*

(12 July 2005). They show that lack of stimulation leads to a wide range of abnormalities. Follow up studies on these children have tragically confirmed this, beyond doubt, as shown in: O'Connor T.G, Zeanah C.H. *Attachment Disorders: Assessment Strategies and Treatment Approaches. Attach Hum Dev* **5** (3): p. 223–44 2003). The Better Care Network reports also show this clearly at: *http://handstohearts.org/wp-content/uploads/2011/04/Global-Fact-Sheet-on-Orphanages_BetterCareNetwork.pdf.*

The brain will simply not grow.

The recent work of Dr. Bruce D. Perry at the Child Trauma Academy using M.R.I. scans actually shows the reduction in size of a child's brain when they suffer from severe sensory-deprivation neglect, relative to that of a healthy child. In some extreme cases there is a 50% difference in brain size. The work of John Bowlby in this area will also provide a rich source of information about the effects of maternal deprivation. His famous W.H.O. report *Maternal Care and Mental Health* was published in 1951. His important work on attachment is covered in: *A Secure Base: Clinical Applications of Attachment Theory* (Routledge London 1988).

Berne identified four different types of strokes:

For a much fuller description and summary of strokes, see the excellent *TA Today* by Ian Stewart and Vann Joines (1987). This remains one of the most succinct descriptions of Transactional Analysis and the essential handbook for all students of this subject.

The experiments of Harry Harlow...

The famous surrogate mother monkey experiments of Harry Harlow showed that monkeys raised alone in an environment without mother and peers, preferred to be with a cloth-covered mother surrogate *without a milk bottle* rather than with a wire-cage surrogate mother that provides a milk bottle, even when hungry. Harlow concluded: *"We did not expect it (the contact comfort of soft mummy) to overshadow so completely the variable of nursing; indeed the disparity is so great as to suggest that <u>the primary function of nursing</u> as an affectional variable is that of <u>insuring frequent and intimate body contact</u> of the infant with the mother. Certainly, Man cannot live by milk alone."* Harlow, H.F. *The maternal Affectional System of Rhesus Monkeys* in Rheingold (ed) *Maternal Behavior in Mammals* (New York: Wiley 1963).

The interesting thing is that they give negative conditional strokes…

Amy Chua's *The battle Hymn of The Tiger Mother* (Penguin 2011) provides a thought provoking insight into how Chinese culture deals with aspirations of excellence and success very differently from western culture.

The famous KIPP charter schools that are springing up all across America.

These schools and their boot camp approach to learning, are described more fully by Malcolm Gladwell in chapter 11 of *Outliers* (2008).

13. THE FIVE HUMAN INTERACTIONS

The different ways in which human beings interact was described by Berne as Structure Hunger.

It is this fundamental hunger for stimulus that decides how we structure our time (Tony Tilney *Dictionary of Transactional Analysis*). Berne actually described six ways of doing this, but I have merged *Activities* with *Pastimes* for simplicity, due to their similarity. For the record, *Pastimes* are more about discussions we have with each other and *Activities* are more about doing things together. There is very little else that separates them in their position between rituals and games. For a fuller description of structure hunger see *TA Today* (Stewart & Joines 1987), chapter 9.

For the purposes of clarity, let us just suppose that our "stroke economy" requires the electrical stimulation of 750 kilowatts a day to our spinal cord for us to be content.

In reality, different people have very different stroke economies. Some people seem to survive on a very low stroke economy, whilst others clearly need a high level. Although it is clear that some people "get away with" less strokes than others, mostly there is a price to pay in health or functionality for a persistently low stroke economy. Folks need strokes and most of us need a basic minimum to get along in life. Humans are not so very disparate in their needs. People with consistently low stroke economies are more likely to suffer health and mental issues. Those of us who work in mental health see this simple correlation on a daily basis.

A poor stroke economy kills....

As long ago as 1915, James H.M.Knox Jr of the Johns Hopkins Hospital noted that, in spite of adequate physical care, 90% of the infants in Baltimore orphanages and foundling homes died within a year of admission; Gardner, L.L. *Deprivation Dwarfism* (Scientific American, 1972). In the same year Dr. Henry Dwight Chapin published a report concerning children's institutions in ten cities. His findings were that infant mortality was 99% with the first year. This wasting away was called "Marasmus." This appalling figure was completely turned around when more staff were brought in so there was time to play, cuddle and talk to the children. The message is clear: without physical and emotional recognition, we die.

The power of sensory deprivation has been common knowledge amongst those regimes involved in torture. The work of Spitz in this field demonstrates clearly the correlation between physical deterioration and the lack of stimulus; Spitz, R. *Hospitalism, Genesis of Psychiatric Conditions in early Childhood* (Psychoanalytic Study of The Child I: 53-74, 1945). Heron identified the fragmentation of the personality that can occur from such deprivation; Heron, W. *The Pathology of Boredom* (Scientific American, January 1957).

GAMES: Summarising game theory into just a few paragraphs has necessitated the omission of much important material. The biggest omission is the contribution of Stephen Karpman. He identified that the easiest way to spot a game is to look for the three major characteristics of any game, namely a **Persecutor**, a **Rescuer** and a **Victim**. If you find yourself in any one of these three roles, or moving between them, then you are likely to be in the middle of a game. In his award winning article Karpman identified these three different roles as present in each game and linked them to the characters in fairy tales; Karpman, S. *Fairy Tales and Script Drama Analysis* (TAB 7, 26 1968). Stewart and Joines (1987) summarise this drama triangle well, in chapter 23.

14. LIFE SCRIPT

Eric Berne's greatest writing about Life Script can be found in *What Do You Say After You Say Hello?* (1972). Two years later, Steiner wrote *Scripts people Live* (1974). An up to date summary of what Life Script means to Transactional Analysts fifty years on can be found in the excellent book *Life Scripts*, (ed. Richard Erskine, 2010).

Yet this is *exactly* what all those involved in the psychological sciences describe.

Claude Steiner (student, colleague and friend of Eric Berne) writes:

Berne postulated that people make decisions in childhood which shape the rest of their life's "script." The concepts that we in Transactional Analysis refer to as "life scripts," "script decisions" and "redecisions" are represented in the wider psychological culture by a widely explored set of concepts; "narratives," "maladaptive schemas," "self-narratives," "story schemas," "story grammars," "personal myths," "personal event memories," "self-defining memories," "nuclear scenes," "gendered narratives," "narrative coherence," "narrative complexity," "core self-beliefs" and "self-concept," which highlight the importance of life stories, myths, plots and characters.
http://analyzingtransactions.blogspot.co.uk.

"By the time he is six, our typical human being has left kindergarten..."
What Do You Say After You Say Hello? (p.97, 1972).

"The child is born free, but he soon learns different."
What Do You Say After You Say Hello? (p.9, 1972).

15. A VERY OLD IDEA

"Someday, someone is going to discover what human living is all about..."
USA T.V. Documentary NET science broadcast 1966.

16. THE LOCATION OF LIFE SCRIPT

The location of Life Script is a massive topic. Whilst most authorities agree that our script began in the Child, there is much debate regarding its presence in the other ego states. It is inconceivable that our template for living is not ubiquitous across the whole psyche. However, for simplicity's sake I place it purely in the Child. There is another very personal reason: such a simple map works effectively in the groups who use *The Fairy Tale Process*, as outlined in Book 3 of *The Psychology of Change series*.

For our purposes we are going to call this part of the Child, "The Script writer"

Most writers agree that it is the problem solving Adult "within the Child" (known as the "little professor" or "A^1") that is responsible for much of our life script. What all writers on the subject agree on is that script is a many layered beast. Berne himself clearly suggests that we simply "download" beliefs in the first two years of life. Attachment theory suggests that we absorb a visceral layer of script from our early bonding experiences. More recently, there has been much fascinating discussion of the importance of these early non-verbal and pre-symbolic foundations of our life script; Cornell, W. in *Life Scripts* (ed. Erskine, 2010).

17. HOW LIFE SCRIPT EVOLVES

For a fuller understanding of this subject, read *TA Today* Stewart & Joines Pt. IV (1987) and *Life Scripts* (ed. Erskine, 2010).

18. DANGEROUS URGES

This tragic story was widely reported in the media. *Guardian*, Tue 14th Jan, 2014

19. WHY WE ALL DO WHAT WE DO

There is much debate regarding what being "script free" actually means. Traditionally, Transactional Analysts regarded becoming "script free" as the aim and purpose of all therapy. More recently, the view has emerged that script is a dynamic thing that continuously evolves. It is my own view that script is always healthy. This is because it is a narrative that defines how we survived in life, and how we continue to survive. Some of it is just outdated and needs rewriting.

BIBLIOGRAPHY

Bentall, R. P.   *Doctoring The Mind* (2009)

Berne, E.   *A Layman's Guide to Psychiatry and Psychoanalysis* (1968)

Berne, E.   *Transactional Analysis in Psychotherapy* (1961)

Berne, E.   *The Structure and Dynamics of Organisation and Groups* (1963)

Berne, E.   *Games People Play* (1964)

Berne, E.   *Principles of Group Treatment* (1966)

Berne, E.   *Sex In Human Loving* (1970)

Berne, E.   *What Do You Say After You Say Hello?* (1972)

Berne, E.   *Intuition and Ego States"* (ed.P McCormick) (1977)

Bowlby, J.   *Maternal Care and Mental Health* (1951)

Bowlby, J.   *A Secure Base: Clinical Applications of Attachment Theory* (1988)

Chua, A.   *The battle Hymn of The Tiger Mother* (2011)

Colby K.M.   *Energy and Structure in Psychoanalysis* (1955)

Domasio, A.   *Descartes' Error: Emotion, Reason, and the Human Brain* (1994)

Erskine, R. (ed.) *Life Scripts* (2010)

Freud, S.   *The Interpretation of Dreams* (1900)

Freud, S.   *Beyond The Pleasure Principle* (1920)

Freud, S.   *New Introductory Lectures* (1933)

Freud, S.   *On Metapsychology* (collection) (1991)

Groddeck, G.   *The Book of the It* (1923)

Gladwell, M.   *Outliers* (2008)

Hargaden, H.   *Ego States* (2003)

Harlow, H.F.   *The Maternal Affectional System of Rhesus Monkeys* Rheingold (ed) (1963).

Lipton, B.   *The Biology of Belief* (2005)

Laplanche, J. & Pontalis, J.B.   *The Language of Psycho-Analysis* (1967)

Pyves, G   *Mavis and I; A Journey of personal Transformation* (2007)

Montagu, A.   *Touching: The human significance of the skin* (1971)

Peters, S.   The Chimp Paradox (2011)

Schiff et al   *The Cathexis Reader* (1975)

Siegal, D. J.   *The Developing Mind: How Relationships and the Brain Interact to Shape Who We Are* (1999)

Stone, M. H.   *Healing the mind* (1997)

Steiner, C.   *Scripts People Live* (1974)

Stewart, I.   *Eric Berne* (1992)

Stewart, I. & Joines, V.   *TA Today* (1987)

Szasz, T.   *The healing word* (1997)

Totten, N.   *Body Psychotherapy - an introduction* (2003)

Tiger, L.   *Optimism; The Biology of Hope.* New York. Simon and Schuster (1979)

Tilney, T.   *Dictionary of Transactional Analysis* (1998)

Viney, W. & King, D. B.   *A History of Psychology* (2003)

Young, J. E.   *Cognitive Therapy for Personality Disorders: A Schema-Focused Approach* (1999)

Zeig, J. K. (Ed.) *The Evolution of Psychotherapy: The Third Conference* (1997)

ACKNOWLEDGMENTS

There is simply not enough space to acknowledge all those people on whose shoulders I have been standing for that part of my life where I believe that I have been at all effective. It would read as a "who's who" of Transactional Analysis, psychoanalysis and psychology.

Even as an experienced Massage therapist, I found that Eric Berne had more to teach me about Massage than all my previous teachers put together. He did this without knowing anything himself about Massage. He did this because of his passion and dedication to understanding what it is that makes us human. I find it remarkable to admit that the person who changed my life more than any other person on the planet is someone I never met. Such is the power of his education and writing. This book would never have been written without his courage, his heroism and his perseverance, even in the face of a life script that must have continually have threatened extinction for letting such brilliance show itself.

I wish to acknowledge all the teachers, therapists, supervisors and colleagues who have been instrumental in my healing, my understanding and my work - you know who you are.

I also wish to thank all the team at Shi'Zen publications; yet again you have dragged me through the fires of your high standard of excellence. Sometimes you did this despite my kicking and screaming.

Finally I wish to acknowledge the constant support, help and encouragement of my dearest friend Geraldine and my loving partner, Ella. Your love and your support keep me afloat in this ocean of life.

ABOUT GERRY

After a brief career in physical and experimental theatre, Gerry graduated in history from Magdalen College, Oxford. He is a U.K.C.P. registered Transactional Analysis Psychotherapist and the founder and creator of The NO HANDS® Massage Therapy System, a unique Transactional approach to Bodywork. Gerry provides advanced training courses for Massage therapists internationally, and runs groups for anyone who is interested in the psychology of change. He is passionate about bringing the power of Transactional Analysis into the homes and lives of as many people as possible. Gerry lives in Hebden Bridge with his partner, Ella, and he has three children who have all managed to grow up far more than he ever did.

www.psychologyofchange.co.uk

ABOUT FRAN

Before becoming a cartoonist Fran was a social work manager. Since taking up his pen 10 years ago his cartoons have been used by over 80 magazines and newspapers in both the UK and Europe. He has been published in PRIVATE EYE, THE TIMES, THE SPECTATOR and NEW STATESMAN as well as having had a regular strip in both THE OBSERVER and THE DAILY TELEGRAPH. Fran lives in Hebden Bridge and is very happily married to Lynette. They have

three children and a dog. When not pretending to work, Fran pretends to do a bit of running and lifting weights. When he has more time he is going to pretend to do some D.I.Y.

www.francartoons.co.uk